Anonymous

O Aster Tou Cheirou Basilikos

Nuncius Christi Sydereus, the star of the Eastern-sages - being a discourse of that star, its nature, conduct and tendency, with the glorious kingdom of the Son of God under the cross

Anonymous

O Aster Tou Cheirou Basilikos
Nuncius Christi Sydereus, the star of the Eastern-sages - being a discourse of that star, its nature, conduct and tendency, with the glorious kingdom of the Son of God under the cross

ISBN/EAN: 9783337294939

Printed in Europe, USA, Canada, Australia, Japan

Cover: Foto ©Lupo / pixelio.de

More available books at **www.hansebooks.com**

Ὁ Ἀστὴρ τοῦ χριστοῦ βασιλικὸς

OR

Nuncius Christi Sydereus.

The STAR of the Eastern-
SAGES.

Being

A discourse of that Star, its Nature, conduct and tendency.

With the Glorious KINGDOM of the Son of God, (now) under the Cross, and shortly at his next appearance to fill the whole Earth.

Also some account of COMETS, and other Signs presaging it.

Numb. 24. 17, 19. *Dan.* 2. 34, 44.

Voetius *de signis.*

A *signis Cæli hujusmodi, paveant Impii.* p. 927.
Prodigia benefica, credentibus; Malefica, & horrifica, incredulis. C. A. Lap. *in Joel* 2. 30.
Quod signum erit iræ Dei Impiis; signum erit perfectæ redemptionis filiis Dei Zanch.

(*de operibus Dei.*)

LONDON,
Printed for *Dorman Newman,* at the *Kings-Arms* in the *Poultrey.* 1681.

CANDID READER.

THE *greatest things God ever did in the world, have ever had Signs and Portents precedaneous: If his doings were Judicial, Tremendious Signs did still presignifie them, if merciful efforts, still some way, ordinary or extraordinary, his wondrous works shew'd that his name was near, to deliver his people, and for the most part the same sign had double signatures and different, as the subject was capable, (like the Sun on wax, and clay) soft or hard. Thus Israels freedom from* Egypt, *and* Pharaohs *Obduracy, and obcæcation, had the same signs and prævious portents, that vastly vary'd in their Issues; they were destroyed,* Israel *delivered, God took these by signs to be his own; the other judg'd by fury pour'd out.*

Now of these signs some are mirandous only; and some miraculous: some the pro-

A 2 *ducts*

To the Reader.

ducts of nature; some preter-or supernatural; some of a convincing nature, as to the wicked (as that hand on Belshazzars wall:) some terrifying, as was that Spectrum that (in Samuels mantle) appeared to Saul, a little ere he fell: and some too are very sweet and comfortable; both as they direct in our way, and support in the hopes of a good event; or else reporting to us some doctrine or duty; the one to be believ'd, the other done. Or lastly (for variety,) some signes are terrene and frequent in this Terrestrial Globe, as in the waters, &c. some more Æthereal, and Cœlestial, and so being seen of more, are more amusing. Of that sort are blazing-stars and Comets.

For those first created stars of God, in their erratile motions in the lower spheres (to the seventh) or those whose fixation is in the eighth story (or chamber) where Ticho-Brahe, and others reason that Star in 1572 was fixt: I have had little (save collaterally) to say; and now have no occasion to discourse at all: Only I wish that this Art of Astronomy, so far as tis capable and possible, by some able naturalist, were reduced to the Holy Scripture and (as Mr. Fr. B. prov'd) fairly deducible from it: its best Phylologia Theologiæ ancillare. Learning, Libraries, and leasure might be well subservient that way

To the Reader.

As to my design, in this Epistolary Preface, to the subsequent discourse: I will onely stay the Reader in a few words of New-stars: somewhat of the present subject, discuss't: and lastly a word of Apology for the Authour.

Now for the first, If any say no new stars are made, God finish't all the host of heaven at first, I say experience in the Providential Regiment of things, makes the Contrary manifest to any observer; we may as truly deny any other new thing: (that in the History of times have serv'd) as portents, in the waters, in the earth, and all over the lower world, and why not also above, in the Firmament? Dare any cavil at Scripture and Experience, this is even affected blindness; was not the Portents in Egypt, *all new? the wonders in the Red Sea, and wilderness, that rain of Manna, and watery Rock all new? the stop of the Sun in* Josh. 10.11. *(by the great faith of* Joshua*) a new work? So that offer of a sign to* Ahaz: *and that grant of two or three to* Hezekiah, *all miraculous, and new? That woman compassing a man, and that blessed birth of the Virgin, all new? and besides 'tis promised* Jer. 33.3. *to be shown, upon his prayer, great and wonderful things that he knew not: and to Zion that he would create Jerusalem a rejoycing. Now to Create is aliquid*

To the Reader.

ex nihilo facere, (*i. e.*) de novo *to make products in the whole frame of Nature, in Heavenly bodies themselves, which never was seen or known before.*

I confess Solomon *said what had been, should be, no new thing: but that's respectively to be took, and with limitation to the natural order and concourse of things; or the habits, or manners of men in his times, (not ours) for since, what mutations have ages seen?* Lactantius *in divers of his works (especially* 7 *li.) tells us, that the very Stars should shoot, alter, fall, and be confounded,* &c. *in our last age.*

Now 'tis a point of Philosophy indeed, to tell the nature of any Star, tho' so long in the view of all wise observers, (or of the Moon that is nearest to us;) and to me it's a poynt of more curiosity, abstruseness & difficulty to tell the Natures, Causes and kinds of these Comets (tho' the use and ends of them are very obvious:) as in Divinity, so in all Arts are Heresies, and so in the Mathematicks *and* Astronomy *are nodes and disceptations as yet indissoluble: It's so in the nature of Comets.* Aristotle *the Master seems unfit to be believ'd of many followers. It may not be then wonder'd at, if in a matter wherein are* tot sententiæ quot capita, *I also may err or stumble in judgment, who thinks Comets are not*

so

To the Reader.

so low as Meteors in the Air, for Nature or Site, exhal'd from the clamy and unctuous vapours of the Earth: it loooks as an improbable thing, that the effect should exceed the cause: Nil dat quod non habet, *that the Earth should produce above it self, bodies (perhaps two or three in a year) so many times (oft hundreds) bigger then it self: but* credat qui vult.

I know it's easier to define what Comets are not, what they are positively to say, is not so easie: To propose then (not impose) as is fair in Schools of Philosophy: I only offer, Why may they not be providential matter fram'd and created of God for the ends proposed, (as the stars at first) to signifie Gods Wrath at hand; for mans sin? and all newly made, as the Rainbow was.

But because I pretend not to any abstrusity of judgment in that enquiry: I say as Noble Picus Mirand.

Philosophia veritatem querit, *Theologia* Invenit, Religio possidet.

That I English thus,
*Philosophy for truth does seek,
   Divinity it finds;
But 'tis possest only by meek
   And most Relogious minds.*

I *am*

To the Reader.

I'm apt to think, were the World fuller of such divine Pious Magicians, *as them of the East,* such enthusiasts *as* Noah *to fear a Flood, and prepare an Ark,* and such Trismegisticks *as* Moses, Abraham *and* Job, (*call them* Fanaticks *or* Seekers, *or what you please*) *there would be both more and better Philosophy then yet is, even with our* Athenian *Academies*.

2. *For the Subject discust :* I freely own my self as many degrees below it, as the sign is above, that portends it : or as that ninth Sphear, (or the Cœlum Empireum) is above this little terrene Globe. For tis the Kingdom of the Son of God, Heir of all things, to whom by deed of Gift the Father has deriv'd power over all flesh, and particularly of these Isles, and the utmost parts of the Earth, Psal. 2. 8, 9. whom all the Angels of God must adore a sublime Subject, above a Ceraphim, and woe is me, that the witnesses to it are so few, nay so many against it, (a sign spoken against (Luk. 2. 34.) about his first, and now at his second coming : that is the cause, the Clergy and Herodians were so tongue tyed, the first out of self and slavish fear: The second from adulation, idolizing an Idumean; that the Romans had substituted over them. Illuminating Truths may better be endured then biting truths : Hence it is that

To the Reader.

that God chose of Fishermen to be his Witnesses; that were men of no name: (and sometimes men exposed of two names) to bear up his name and Glory before the Great of the Earth.

This is my Subject, which, (with Zions Glory and Controversie,) is so rarely preacht, or toucht by the men, that (perhaps) do confess the same in our times; and those that are the regent and triumphant Sons of the Church, are instead of it, set to Preach, and Print, and vend the poyson of horrid Blasphemy against the Lord and the Decalogue, for the wounding of Jo. Calvin, and other Reformers for his sake; or rather Christs, whom they serve.

As contiguous to that I do also insist on the judgments that preceed, and the subsequent changes that use to subserve that design: for that now tottering Antichristian Throne of Iniquity, and Christs Scepter of equity are so inconsistent, so contestant with each other, that neither will the one fall and give place, nor can the other take place, without judicial concussions, as Herod here felt; tho' it first cost a sad Exile to Jesus and (his Friends) Jos. and Mary, and the blood of 14000 Infants for his sake: (so it's said,) not sparing his own Son too: so jealous and tickle is the point of Succession, and so cruel

Fathers

To the Reader.

Fathers oft Kings are to their Subjects, if Christ have any birth, or plea with them.

Subservient to both the foresaid points, This new Star took its Being, Rise, and unusual Motion, not from East to West, as Comets mostly do, (and Origen *calls it so,) but from East to North, and from* Jerusalem *(the North,) to* Bethlehem *in the South; and hence our poynt gets its Basis layd, somewhat large and general, to give scope enough to the design, (that our late Comet incited me to pursue) in the 4 following Treatises, and to comprehend both the use of Comets (so rarely handled in a Theologick way;) and also the influences, constellations, and conjunctions of other Stars, first created, all which jump, and (in eodem tertio) agree. (viz.) in one Maxim of invincible truth, that towards great mutations to succeed on Earth, prodigious phænomenas do in Comets, &c. preceede in the Heavens.*

Now thirdly, 'tis in this that I make a short Apology: To those that think 'twere more profitable to treat of other theames; to them I say are not the works of God to be useful in our Doctrine, as well as his word? especially when Prodigious, and to be sought out of all that had pleasure therein? May we not read in them our call to repent, and prepare, when signs of fire are set up.

If

To the Reader.

If any say things are but left in obscurity? I grant we Prophesie but in part; the Text is in some things hard to Fathom, which may plead the Authours excuse, voluisse sufficiat, *more then a dozen Authors I read, many found cited by others, onely three Doctors I read on the Text, and one* (i.e.) Cyprian *(sayes Mr.* Ward *) preacht on a like Comet (if ever any like to this.)*

Do any think me too near the quick. I say thats the life of Preaching; I am much below it, what ere others be: If I (then living) had singl'd out (as once Act. 4. 25. 27. *the Apostles did name)* Herod, *and* Pontius Pilate, *from* Psal. 2: 1. *dare any impeach them for too close reflections? boldness is brave for God, adulation pernicious to Princes: and a just wise reprover, on an obedient ear, a most excellent ornature.* Prov. 25. 11, 12, 13. *'Twas once said,* Da Ambrosios *&* habebemus Theodosios. *But if I say not (as* Nathan *to* David *) thou* Ch. Lewis, *or* Jam-art *the man meant, am I not safe? Alas Sirs, shall our God be blasphemed, mockt and spit at: Christ made a servant of Rulers, nay but a titular King; blood be spilt as waters, oppressions practised under the sacred Covert of a Dukes Coronet, an* Episcop. Mytre, *or a Golden Cap: (that I say not a red*

To the Reader.

red Hatt?) and must faith and sacred Oaths be swallow'd (as Monkeys do) and all slipt, the bounds and banks of the people be tipt down as Nine pins; the power of Parliaments vacat: Horid Conspiracies abetted, and father'd, as Londons *fire;* Ireland *be gap't at. &c. and it must be thought not onely a diminution of our glory to be reprov'd; but an affront to crave relief; (as* Israel *of Pharaoh) we in this may sit down and see or say as* Israel *in* Exod. 5. 19. *or those in a like case,* Judg. 19. ult. *Some called fathers in the world, prove so indeed to poor Protestants, (witness the Rampant Mounsieur:) for while he lives (and acts so) his poor Protestant Subjects will never inherit Christs purchase, and their birth-right.*

If any say the Press now has too exorbitant a Liberty, to vend stories and lies: I answer, I'm sorry for the lyes: on them be the guilt that first coyned them; but yet glad too that the press and truth are not opprest by any barking and pernicious Currs: that used as Doeg *(or* Cerberus*) to sit at the gates to obstruct the free course of truth. And for the two particulars (in the 4 part) that of one whose eyes fell out, and the tother of Mr.* Claud, *in* Paris. *I had the first by a worthy man, and so the second by a Minister, though this is differently reported; for*

the

To the Reader.

the substance, it was in the case of Religion that abuse was offer'd, but yet his life was preserv'd.

If any object the Authors not owning his work by name, I say, the thing he's willing to own; and being his first Fruit, he wholy dedicates it to the Lord, and his Auditory; where it cannot be hid; craving the Readers excuse for the meanness of parts, and privacy of Circumstances, at present reads him a Lecture of modesty, and so desiring to be less known to others, and more to himself. So prayes this may end to thy profit.

Si bene quid scripsi gloria Christe tua est.

Erratr

ERRATA.

Candid Reader. A Book without Errata's is not easy to find, those that cloud the sense the Author hath revised and expung'd to the utmost (as his health and strength gave leisure) yet if escapes by interlines in the Copy be, they will not be imputed, I hope. There's a great difference indeed twixt Books publisht by the Authors exact Notes, and the Auditers hasty characters. the First he uses not: the latter is his excuse; for the Accents, some Lattin Words, Marg. or Comaes, and Periods; I trust the Printer will obtain the civility of pardon, or a Pen to amend them.

Si male quid scripsi; sit mihi, culpa~~~~ Vale.

Phil. Melancth.

Certum est, multas in Elementis, ab astris Mutationes oriri, & —lumen celeste magnam vim habere.
Novit deus omnia solus — (trahantur.
Quæ sint, quæ fuerint, quæ mox ventura Omnia hæc signa, esse Imminentis Iræ Dei, quam necesse est quoquo modo possumus,) ut & anunciemus, & predicimur. Tert. ad Scap. *prodigia sunt* τὰ τῶ Θεῶ χηρύγματα. Euse.

Dr. Jackson cites Herodotus. *Quoties Ingentes sunt Eventuræ calamitates —solent signis prenuntiari.*

Prodigia sunt signa divinæ admonitionis, ut excitemur ad timorem Dei, & caveamus per resipiscentiam, futura incomoda. Brentius.
Ipsis signis & portentis, pii se consolantur, quia sciunt sibi illa in bonum cooperatura, & lætantur, quia sciunt esse patris sui exercitum. Petr. Mart.

The Analysis of the first Part
Chap. 2. ver. 1.—12.

2 Parts in't { 1. *Christs Blessed Nativity*, per totum.
{ 2. *Herods cursed enmity*, v. 3, 7, 8, &c.

In the First, 3 things are Considerable.

{ 1. *The Time*: Herods Reign. v. 1.
{ 2. *The Adjuncts concuring*, v. 2. &c. Luk. 2. 1.
{ 3. *The Place*, and that proved by Micah 5. 2.

In the Second, (Collating Matthew with Luke, chap. 2. 1.—40.) 4 *Adjuncts*, (or *Circumstances*) occur.

{ 1. *Angels Annunciation, and Acclamation.*
{ 2. *John Baptists Nativity.*
{ 3. *The Shepherds Revelation of him.*
{ 4. *The Wisemens Visitation.* In this (yet) observe further, them 4 things.

{ 1. *Their Stile or Title*, Magi.
{ 2. *Their Countrey*, the term, (a quo.)
{ 3. *The Inquiry*, the ground and end of it, v. 2.
{ 4. *Their Colloquy about it with Herod.*

Yet once more particularly in v. 2. observe 2 parts.

    1. *The Matter.*
    2. *The Motive.*

{ The 1. Notes the quality of *Christs Nativity*, 2. the *Object*, 3. *The ubi.*
{ 2. *The Motive*, A *Star*: the predicate, have seen.
{ 3. *The Effects.*
{ 4. *The Site* (in the East.)

Now in the Effects noted,

{ 1. *Reverence, or Piety.*
{ 2. *Sedulity in a long journey.*
{ 3. *Charity, presenting,* { 1. Gold.
                                  { 2. Frankincense.
                                  { 3. Myrrhe.

———— (Dona ferunt) ————
(Aurum, thus, Myrrham, regiq; hominiq; deoq;)

This

The Analysis.

This Star is described,
1. By *the Situation or point,* East.
2. By *its End, or Effect,* { 1. To *Guide them.*
   2. To *Glad them.*
3. By *its* 5 *Properties,* (Novi Cometæ Instar.)
   { 1. *Seen.*
   { 2. *On the Day-time.*
   { 3. *Lost.*
   { 4. *Seen again.*
   { 5. *In the lowest Region.*

Matth.

Matth. 2. 2, 9, 10.

IT is an observation of *Aretius* (*a*) upon this place, when God hath some great work, some glorious King or Kingdom to exhibit in the World; he shews it by some prodigious Celestial Sign or Star, or other. It is said in the *Psalmes*, *The Workes of the Lord are great*, (as well as his Word) *sought* (*b*) *out, of all them that have pleasure therein.* Among which works some of them are stupendious and great; some mysterious and inscrutable; some are sweet and comfortable, (and all very useful;) But some of them are exceeding wonderful and terrible.

There are Terrestrial Terribles, and Celestial Terribles. There are Terrible signs in the Sun, signs in the Moon; (that

---

(*a*) *Majorum virorum ortus, & occasus, in cælo, prodigiis quandoq; denuntiantur.* (*b*) *Psal.* 111. 2. *cum.* 107. *vet.*

turned into Darkness, (c) this into Blood) before the great and notable Day of the Lord. And there are also signs as Terrible in the Stars; there are Heart-shakes, Earth-shakes, and Heaven-shakes, as our Saviour himself prophesied in *Luk.* 21. 25, 26.

I have had occasion (you know) to discourse to you, in my way formerly about the Salvation of God; The Voice of which, sometimes, is very loud on Earth; but when it won't be believed there, then God sets up Preachers in Heaven, and makes it as loud there: but very hard to understand.

Now there being a new Kingdom, a Kingdom of Christianity, Christ being the Head, to be exalted in the World; God, by a (d) new-made Star, is pleased to pronounce and promulgate the same in the Text; which is the sole Text that speaks of a new (†) Star in the whole Bible.

I have therefore chosen it, not with a design to deliver Astrological Doctrine, nor to place my Pulpit in the Heavens, and read a Lecture of the Laws of the Hea-

---

(c) *Joel.* 2. 28. *Act.* 2. 20. (d) *Stella nova & peculiaris creata dici necesse est.* Aret. (‡) *Tanta cura digni sunt pii, ut etiam sydera illis & angeli inserviant. Id. Ibid. in locum.*

vens;

vens, or of Astronomy; (though it be said, both *Abraham*, *Moses*, and *Job*, and other of the Saints were excellently skilful and learned therein;) Much less will I be so Atheistical, either (on the one hand) to Preach up the necessity of second Causes alone, and self-persisting; or (on the other hand) to deny the efficacy and infallible certainty in the Succession of them by the governance of the great Cause of Causes, God himself.

Now the Scripture that I have singled out, is a part of the History of our blessed Lord's poor, low (e) Nativity; born of a Virgin of mean obscure descent, but the Glory of it not fully known: the supposed Son of *Joseph*, by Calling, a Carpenter: under the servitude of the *Roman* Emperour, *Augustus Cæsar*. For as great as she was, unto her Native Town *Bethlehem* must she come to be taxed, so was deliver'd (there wanting room in the house) (*Romes* great Men, must have their Taxes paid, whatever Poverty it cost their Subjects) She's glad to lodge her self in a Stable; and the Child, (for want of a Cradle) is laid in a Manger. When it became

---

(e) *Nil hic regale patet, omnia vilia, & sordida sunt, caula potius quam aula reperitur.*

B 2 Herod

Herod rather, as *Augustus Cæsar* (f) to vail his Crown to his Footstool; as well as the wise Men (Kings some take them to be) from the East.

This Scripture it self (so far as the 12th. verse) reports two things.

1. Our Lord's blessed Nativity, though poor.

2. And *Herods* cursed immanity, (g) seeking to stifle and murther the first appearance of the blessed Babe of Glory. All exhibition of Christ, that in the Cradle at the first coming; that to the Crown, the next and second coming; that into the Heart, into the World, (his spiritual comings betwixt these two) I say, all these appearances and smallest exhibitions of Christ, are a kind of terrour, and occasion of enmity to wicked men.

This first branch, where my work chiefly lyes; the Nativity of our blessed Lord is celebrated divers wayes; One while, by Angels singing blessed Songs: *Glory to God on high: on earth Peace, good Will towards*

(f) So Pol. Virg. out of Orosius, *sayes, the day Christ was born, Augustus Cæsar Proclaimed, that no man ever after should call him Lord. Manifesto presagio majoris dominatus qui tum in terris ortus esset.* lib. 4. cap. 1. (g) *More of the Analysis see before the first page.*

Men.

Men. (For, never comes Chriſt into the World, the Heart, the Houſe: but he brings good Will.) Celebrated by the Shepherds that were feeding their Flocks by Night: theſe alſo were guided to the knowledge of this bleſſed Birth, this Author of Divinity. And laſtly, Celebrated by the wiſe men; and ſaid, to come (ſome ſay) from *Perſia* (*h*); and then it may be but about eight or nine hundred and odd Miles. Others ſay, from *Arabia Felix*, and that's (*i*) ſuppoſed to be about twelve hundred and forty odd Miles. Sure 'twas a long way to come to one Sermon or Sight. Oh how few go ſo far as the Eunuch of *Candace*! as the Queen of *Sheba*! as theſe wiſe men! That is the beſt and ſweeteſt Chriſt that hath the moſt pains taken for him.

Theſe by their name, or employ, are here ſtyled *Magi*, which is to ſignifie wiſe men, riſing from a root (*k*) *Haga* הגה In the *Hebrew* it (*l*) ſignifies deep thoughtfulneſs and Meditation.

(*h*) *At leaſt* 520 *Miles.* (*i*) *Bunting ſayes it was about* 920 *Miles from* Suſan, *an Accademy; but that* Zeba(*the likelier place*) *was it,* 1248 *Miles to the South-Eaſt.* (*k*) *Murmurare, muſſitare alii meditare.* (*l*) *Others ſay a* Perſian, *others Greek term.*

From which Term you may conclude, (as Authors also agree with me) that there is a twofold Magick; there is a Diabolical Art to seek Wisdom, which is sometimes exerted by the wicked and lawless divining by the Stars; a Doctrine, which God never made known. And there is a lawful Magick, which is by the discovery of Gods Holy Will, either by the Law of the Heavens and the works of God; or by the law of the Word, or some Revelation from God. These were the men, this, their Occupation.

How they should come by the knowledge of this Star, it not uneasie to resolve; for the text tells you, *we have seen his Star*, in the East, ἐν τῇ ἀνατολῇ. Or, as some read, in his Rising, *We have seen his Star in its Rising*; which makes some to think that this was above a year before: for it must require some time for their Journey. And therefore the holy Babe, and Parents, were again returned to dwell in *Bethlehem*, and had no better lodging than the first. But it is not so easie to resolve how they should come by this knowledge; but so much as Authors can by their conjectures help us, or I by reading of them, we shall now easily declare. There are two eminent Doctors have cited one of the antientest of the Philosophers,

losophers, named *Chalcidius*, (m) who a little after the time of Christ, wrote concerning this Evangelist and about this Star. By which you may see, it was notified to Heathen then. And, faith he, (citing the latin out of it) there is a more holy History (meaning this of the Evangelist) which we have read, which signifies to us of a blessed new-made Star. Therefore the discovery (being King of the *Jewes*) was made known unto the wise men. He calls them of the *Persians*, others of the *Arabians*, and others of the *Chaldeans*; (for they might be mixed.) And both those Doctors (Dr. *Hammond*) upon the place, (a learned Critick in the *Eastern* Language) and another of our City, preaching upon some part of this text (Dr. *Gell*) both cite *Chalcidius*.

(m) Dr. Rob. Gell, Dr. Hammond *in locum*, says thus, *Est autem venerabilior & sanctior Hystoria quæ prohibet ortum stellæ insolitæ destensam dei venerabilis ad humanæ servationis & rerum mortalium gratiam: quam à Chaldæis observatam fuisse testantur qui deum nuper natum muneribus venerati sunt.* There is also an holier History that mentions a certain, and unusual Star that foretold the descent of the most venerable God seen, and by the Magi presented with gifts, &c.

B 4 And

And of this East Countrey they say, there was for many hundred of years, a Society of Philosophers, or such as studied wisdom; (for the word signifies so.)

And having no Scripture, but what they had by Tradition, they studied the Law, or motions of the Heavens. And particularly (citing (n) father *John Chrysostom*) there was a city called *Seth* in the East, in which this Society lived: and there continued many ages successively (twelve of them) being under a perpetual Vow devoted to that Study; until *Balaams* Prophesie should be brought to pass, about that Star of *Jacob*, as *Numb.* 24. 17.) For by the help of that Prophesie, or by the Travel of the *Jewes*, or by the fetching and buying of the Merchandize, of Frankincense and Myrrh (which was always used in their incense) or by the holy Ghosts oracle, or by some other works of *Daniel*, (o) or the holy Prophets; knowledg was got, that there was a blessed Star to arise in the later end of the four Thousand years of the World. For though *Balaam* is expresly call'd by *Attersol* a very wicked Conjurer, yet he had a very glorious true Prophesie of the Messias.

(n) *See more in Dr. Gell on the place, pag* 5. *n.* 3.
(o) *Known by the Captivity and dispersion to* Chaldea.

There

There shall come a Star out of Jacob, and a Scepter shall rise out of Israel, and shall smite the corners of Moab, and destroy (or (q) unwall) all the Children of Sheth, Numb. 24. 17. Out of this, or by some such like means, or by some peculiar knowledge, Instinct, Oracle, or Angel given them, with sedulity and diligence, in searching out the Laws of the Heavens, knowledge was attained. Or at least (if none of these satisfie) it must be concluded (for further I may not Conjecture) that God made some Divine Revelation and discovery (r) to these poor Studious Creatures, that there should certainly now arise the Star of Jacob.

But so it was, and so is the Text: for the question implyed it; *where is he that is born King of the Jewes?* As if they should say, we are well assured, and no way doubt (by the Lawes of our Art) of this risen Star, and by the knowledge we have attained, that there is a certain King newly born in *Judea*, and brought forth into the World; that the God of Heaven hath set up a sign of his first coming. Which makes one Author to collect, if there was such a Star,

---

(q) *as H. A. reads it.* (r) *Perhaps by an Angel, so Dr. Hammond in locum.* 6.

attending

attending the first coming of Christ, in his debility and low condition; how much more may many be expected to attend and precede his second, and last coming. Therefore say they, having heard this in our land, knowing this is the Metropolis *Jerusalem*; having heard of this famous City, and the Kings thereof; now we are come to make more enquiry after that King of the *Jews*; We are satisfied he is no mean Person, (whatever his present condition is) but he is born a King, and he shall certainly come to great honour at last.

Now here's a question put, *ver.* 2. and it puzzles both the wise men and Scribes of *Jerusalem*, the most learned of them? and also Plagues the heart of *Herod* with fear; For certainly (thinks he) my Usurpation (*s*) will down, if there be a King that's born to't, and his Right will be up.

Now it so fell out, that whiles these wise men step aside, (and some think, out of their way: For it was about to *Bethlehem*, (*t*) to go by *Jerusalem*) they mist their

---

(*s*) *He being an* Idumean, *of Esau's Stock.* (*t*) *See Bishop* Hooper *his Comment of their Errour in Mr.* Fox *cited aptly by Mr.* Trapp *in locum.*

enquiry

enquiry there, and therefore go out, and presently the Star appears again, as you find in the two latter Verses, 9, 10. the effect of which is reported. When they saw the Star, they rejoyced with exceeding great Joy. (*v*)

Now when I first thought of this Scripture, I only designed to single out one particular, relating to this Star, for the driving on of the great design of the late Subject I was upon: the Signes of Salvation, which God sets; sometimes terribly in the Heavens; sometimes in the Earth, sometimes in the Luminaries; both in the lesser Luminaries the Stars, and also in the greater.

But because all Christ's fragments are to be gathered, and not lost, I will briefly pick up some few Notes, which are Collateral, Profitable, and not far from my purpose and design, and fairly dispatch them, or give you but a taste of them, and then proceed, at least, to an entrance of what I intend.

1. Now the first thing which is observable here for Doctrine, is from the name

---

(u) ἐχάρησαν χαρὰν μεγάλην σφόδρα.

that

that is given here; They are called wise men, (now so indeed;) Their work they set themselves to, is to enquire after Christ.

Hence you may note,

That it is the greatest point of Wisdom, and fit for all sorts that would have that name; to make diligent enquiry after Christ.

He that's not acquainted with the Son of God, will certainly be deservedly called the greatest of Fools. This is the true Wisdom, the Wisdom of the Cross, and the Crucified Saviour; and to know him, and him crucified. If there be any of us that desire to be wiser than our selves formerly, or than others, or than our Teachers, and the Scribes; we must make this our Sedulity and care, to search after Christ.

The second thing that I note from this Text, is this, They came, some say, eight hundred miles the first going; and some say, a thousand and odd, (according to the conjecture of the place, which authors give); and the greatest is most likely, because in that Country was only Frankincense

kincense and Myrrh, as the (*x*) Heathen Poets themselves observe; But this I will only glance at, and observe, That

   2. *Where Christ is savingly reveal'd, no cost, or pains is deem'd too great, for his sake.*

And for long Journeys, see the third Note, *pag.* 14.

Nor could it be void of hazard to tell of a King in *Herods* Ear, and Reign, As one says, (*y*) *Quæstio plena periculi, & summi stuporis; quid hoc erat, nisi Herodem negare dejicere, & novum regem Proclamare; quod capitale profecto erat.* Yet these boldly predicate of a new King born to the *Jews*. The profest *Jews* grown stupid; *Deus peregrinos hos testes regni Christi excitavit, & non sine prodigio, novam enim stellam, novi & magni quid portendere ex arte sua, Intelligebant.* So far he.

(*x*) *Ezek.* 27. 21, 22. *Arabici odores. Thuri, preter Arabiam, nullis. Thurea verga sabeis.* Virgil. (*y*) *Parei in locum. pag.* 413. *Col.* 2.

3. *That*

3. *That it is a great Duty, and very commendable, to go far to seek Christ.*

From Sea to Sea was a long way; *Amos* 8. 12. and yet the length of *Judea* did not extend above two hundred and forty or fifty miles, from *Dan* to *Bersheba*; and the breadth not much above fifty, from *Gath-hepher Jonas* Town, unto *Joppa*. And yet the text saith in *Amos* the 8. 12. they should wander from Sea to Sea, and should not find it; yet all that was not so far, as the *Magi* came.

Sirs, I tell you, from the Multiplicity of Preachers that God hath set up in the Church-heaven, (and yet upon Earth) shining Stars; (for Ministers are called Stars, sometimes) are not the least of the blessings of our Age; and sure 'twould be one of the greatest Judgments that could befall us, to go a great way to seek a Sermon, and not find it.

So must the Mercy be a great Mercy, though it be a great way to go for't and a long time to find: no cost is too much, nor no way too arduous, no Journey too long, no difficulties too great, no hunger too heavy to bear, no pained feet in the Wilderness (say forty years together) to find the promised Land, or Rest, that's Christ.

The

The fourth thing that *I* glance at here, is plain in the second Verse: [*He was born a King.*]

Christ was a King assoon as ever he was born. History tells us of one that was Crowned on the Mothers Belly, before he was born, that was only an humane, Chrsts was a Divine Royalty.

In the eighth of *Proverbs*, we read of this true wisdom of the Father; the Son of God: it is so said, he was by him from everlasting, there's his Divinity, *ver.* 23. always with him, rejoycing in the habitable parts of the Earth, here's his Humanity, *ver.* 25, 30, 31. delighting in the Sons of men. 'Twas not so long a Journey the wise men came ; but Christ from the Father, coming into the World, made a longer: and all out of his love, so by leaving and condescent from his glory, he merited in the Humane nature, a greater accession of Regal Glory. There is no Journey too long, no pains and cost too great for love. Of all the misteries, I have most wondred at this, how these poor Creatures, that had no more, (that we visibly find in our Text) but the language of a Star to preach to them, should thence conjecture, that Jesus was a King assoon as ever he was born. Such is the occult, and mysterious way of

the

the Revelation of Chrift. For he was a King before, declared of God : *I have set my King upon my holy Hill of Sion. Pfal. 2. 7. I will declare the Decree: the Lord hath said, thou art my son this day have I begotten thee.* But now alfo thefe came from the uttermoft parts of the Earth, and they owne the Kingdome of Chrift. Shall we that have heard of him, that have read of him, that have pretended to him, that have preached for him, that have believed his Royalty and Glory, be lefs refolv'd Proteftants than thefe were (z) ? They confeft him born, the King of the *Jews*; and though he had not then any actual Regency over them (for they were now under the *Romans*) yet afterward, it was by the defignment (a) and decree of the Father that he fhould be both King of *Jew*, and *Gentile*, and gather all the Children of God into one. But,

Fifthly, (to haften) By the little acceptance of, as well as the little knowledge that they had concerning Chrift here among them. You may thence obferve,

---

(z) *Pareus calls the* Magi *Primitiæ gentium.*
(a) *Pfal.* 2. 9, 10. *Ifa.* 49. 6. *Joh.* 11. 52.

5. That

That a People may live near and vnder the Exhibition, and Preaching of Christ, daily and yet remain ignorant of him, for no locall litteral Notions will serve.

These poor Creatures had more practical real knowledge (that had but so little *Syderean* light to teach them) then the *Jews*. The *Jews* were turned Heathens, the Heathens true *Jews*. *Rom.* 2. *ult.* The men of the East the true Lovers of Christ; and the men of *Jerusalem* fallen from him. It is very possible, that one may be near Christ in respect of abundance of Revelation, and yet have nothing of Christ revealed in their Hearts, much said, and little known; much taught, and little learned; much knowledge, and little practice; less Love. Neither *Herod*, nor that Sect of *Herodians* (for indeed, all *Jerusalem* were almost of that Sect) (†) did believe a word of what these Phanatick wise men did report; talk of a Child born a King, when there is one possest?

Fifthly, Observe what deep enmitie, (covered over with Hypocrisie) *Herod* was guilty of, in reference to Christ. For he enquired diligently of the wise men what time the Star appeared.

Sometime they must have for their Jour-

(†) Being [*homines ad servitutem parati*,as one says.

ney; by the guidance of this Star they were brought to *Jewry*: Up to *Jerusalem* they came; *Herod* no sooner hears on't; but (whereas the Doctrine of a Saviour should rejoyce the whole World) it only affrights the Court. It is said, though of another (a 2d.) of his name, that he desired much to see Jesus. And *Herod*, when he saw him with his Men of War, set him at naught, (*b*) the 23. *Luke* 11. So does this *Herod.* But that's not all.

 6. *Though the Language was to worship, the end and design was to worry and destroy Christ.*

Enquire diligently where the Babe, the young Child is, and bring me word, that I may come and worship him; as you find in the 7, 8. *verses*, but the t other was the thing he intended. Which makes one Auther, it is *Aretius* his (*c*) passage: Seith he, there is one thing in his mouth, but there's another thing in his heart; he pretends to worship, but intends to Murther, Massacre

---

 (*b*) Luk. 23. 8, 11. *But set him at naught, at the sight of him.* (*c*) Herodes *certe aliud in ore, sed aliud in pectore —— clausum habet. Sanguine fundata est Ecclesia, sanguine Nata, sanguine succrevit, anguine, finis erit.* (*Pareus.*)

          and

and destroy, for it appeared so at last. And therefore this Star did presage both good and evil, (as you'l see by and by,) for there were so many of the poor Children lost their lives; the first Martyrs for Christ.

O! how hard a thing it is to ingratiate a holy Jesus, and a wicked man! (I had almost said, more) a wicked King. For out of doubt *Herod* was so; he was so, take it for granted; He was of a wicked stock that 2000 years almost had been the plague of Gods people, I don't know how many ages. For he was an *Idumean* of the stock of *Esau*: he came to't by insinuation and flattery, he was exalted there by the *Roman* power, he was kept in and defended by them.

The *Roman* Law and Yoak was upon *Israel* at this time; yet he pretended respect and love to their worship and Temple, and gaue gifts towards it; but all this while a real Enemy, (but a hidden) to Christ. Or (as the Phrase in one Author is) he made it his work to lay crafty Plots and insinuations, in a subtle and deceitful way, to find out Christ, and rather then not kill him, he would Murther all the Infants about that Age. But,

In the next place we may observe, the wise men, when they came to the place, had been conducted by the Star all along, and at last found the place of the Blessed Babe. It notes to you.

> 7. *That though it be difficult to seek, yet it is desireable and pleasant to see Jesus, very pleasant.*

On this Note, O how long did you once hear! God, by his Spirit preach it over again to you. I pass it.

8. You may observe, They came to the place, and they offered Gold, Frankincense and Myrrh, and worshipped him. (*d*)

> *That Jesus is a King that deserves all Homage, and Fealty, and Worship and Duty to be given him, from all his Subjects and Servants.* And

9. Observe, *In what a low Condition the Lord Jesus at first exhibited himself into the World.*

O the blessed way and Wisdom of God in this thing! He was not pleased to come forth at first, like some great *Monarch*; He was pleased to make his Friends but

---

(*d*) *In the Greek.* προσκυνήσω, *did cap, or bow at's feet as Spaniels*, ver 8:

few,

few, his Parents mean and poor, his house a Stable; his Company, the Beasts: his Cradle the Manger, and (if one may be critical,) old Clouts for his Swadlings, (old soar rags,) all which was continued in this low state, (*e*) during his own life, and so along, on purpose to teach the Disciples of the Crucified Jesus, all humility.

Mr. *Burroughs* cites *Chrysostom* (*f*) that says wouldst thou be cloathed in Silks? Remember the bands of *Paul*. But then, (say I,) remember the Swathes of Christ. See, and look what a poor wretch art thou! he was a Babe of Glory, what a high state thou livest in! all rich Curtains, rich Arras, rich Hangings, and the like. The Glory and Grandeur of this World, and the Glory and Humility of Christ, are so vastly different. O how should the Doctrine of the Cross, and a Crucified Jesus, better teach Humility to his followers! And yet,

In the Tenth place you may also observe how wonderfully God guided the Wisdom of these Eastern men, to behold an inward

---

(*e*) ἤσπαρ γανωμένον. Luk. 2. 7, 12. *In vilibus & veteribus indumentis.* (*f*) Moses *Choice*, pag. 85. *Velles sericis indui, memor esto Pauli carceris, & vinculorum, vis odoramenta coopta illius lacrimas, et hæc deformitatem putabis.* Chrys. Homil *in* Colos. &c.

Celestial Glory in this low and miserable and despised condition. Hence learn we

10. *Wherein lies the true Wisdom, for a poor Soul, to prize a (g) despised Christ:* When he comes to be exalted, he won't need to be beholding to us for honour. But to prize a Crucified Jesus, and to plead for him as the Thief on the Cross; this man hath done nothing amiss, nothing, *Luk.* 23. 41. ἐδὲν ἄτοπον ἔπραξε, nonot awry. You shall alwaies observe it, those are the true Heirs, and Co-heirs of Christ in the Kingdom, that are so Spiritually agreed, and reconciled to all his low despised Conditions. Seest thou Christ in the poorest Member, in the meanest place, in the most despicable Cottage, in the wofullest Sheep-Coat, O prize him: as it is said in one place, he went into *Bethany*, and lodged there. But *Bethany* was a poor (h) mans House, for Sheep-Coats or Cauls, more then dwelling. And therefore it is as much as tosay, he cauled there; that is, he lodged among the Sheep-cribbs. You see the low estate of themost high Son of God. And,

---

(g) Stellas note is good, *Beata virgo vili stabulo sedit, & jacet; sedquod homines negliunt Cives celestes, honorant, & Inquirun.* (h) *As* Bethany *signifies.* So Luke 21.38. ηὐλίζετο, i. e. *he cauled or soulded there, as* 10.10.1.

11. (That

11. (That I may go no further; and yet reading *Aretius*, that pious grave man, goes to the number of seventeen, in excellent, sweet, and profitable notes, (on this text and context) but I go not so far.)

The Twelfth and last is this, *That God makes known sometimes much of his mind, and Sons Glory by new Stars, or prodigious Comets.*

And this lets you see (in short) what the Text points to: what it was that guided the wise men so many hundred Miles: what it was that carryed the tydings of a new King to the Magi in the East. And according to this, I shall endeavour, (not barely by the light (so much) of the dark bodies in the Heavens; as by the help, and candle of the Scripture, and the guidance thereof to make known something out of the works of God; as formerly, we have preached out of his word. Now as touching the Stars, there are two sorts. Old created, new created. so divers grave Authors call it. Of the former there are the fixed, and moveable stars. This is said of them all in the first Creation; they shall be for signs, and for seasons (*Gen.* 1.14.) for dayes, and years. Signs of coming events that was the Creators end. Of these new ones, whereof this in the Text was one, (and a strange one) something had need to be spoke which may be for the plainest, and the meanest vulgar understanding, as well as the most-wise. If you were as learned as the wise men were; God (it seems) would teach them by the Stars, that had not the word, or had but barely the heresay of it. There are various wayes of Gods making known his will unto the Sons of men, there are some ordinary, there are some extraordinary; there are some things made known by his word, there are others by his works. But whether by the one, or the other, there is a secret impress or influence of his holy Spirit, concurrent, which makes the medium effectual to the end. But in this, I shall be too general.

As for these stars we read in Scripture (for there we'l mainly consult) concerning them, that they have their signatures, as God in the first Creation decreed (*Gen.* 1. 15.) their dominion.(†) We read that they have their weapons : the starrs fought in their courses against *Sisera* and *Jabin*, *Judges* 5. 20. We read of their (*i*) constellations which (I think) answers to that, we call our conjunctions; in which, they

---

(†) *Job.*38.33. (*i*) Isa. 13. 1c. 2 *King.* 23. 5. *(? as some the* 12 *Signs.* seem

seem to concenter and concurre, in the order and course they take, (by the law of their maker) to declare, and point out (as second causes) that there is something to be brought forth in the world.

We read again, of the impressions they have upon the heart of man (mark *David*, how spiritual his heart was, to learn humility, out of the starrs.) When I consider, the Moon and the Stars (he goes no higher) which thou hast ordained, Lord what is man, saith he? in *Psal.*8.3. As if he had said, thou hast not pent thy self in vain in such a glorious beautious canopy (with all the starrs) bespangled; and tho, they have no need to defend thee, yet they preach to us humility; Lord, what is man? We read yet again, in the 19 *Psal. ver.* 3. *There is no language where their* line and word is not heard. *(their words,* (mark ye:)

Why then they have lines, and words. Lines, by which they point out our Center, by which God their maker indicates; And words, by which, they speak their makers will; And there is no language (how remote soever) where their words are not heard. The Stars, (where other means were not wanting) were certain Preachers, and Publishers of the mind and will of
God,

God; unto those that are dutiful and wise observers Now when all these ordinary wayes & Preachers will not attain the right end, why then, God usually makes some new thing, and is pleased to place some new Pulpit, in the heavens, and set up some new starre; of which, *Alstedius (k)* gives us 154, in his History of them; and another writer (though I have not seen the authour) does report all the stars (new Coments I mean) since the Creation. Thus I have led you unto the general intimation of our design, in which will lye the solution of three or four questions.

And I hope, if you'l call it a digression, yet it is no transgression, to handle this kind of learning for once, in three or four Questions for the *substratum* of our second Discourse; I only add in *Janu*. 1661. an Infant twelve times cry'd in the womb; Woe to *Denmark*, and he (*l*) adds. These Cœlestial signs portend some great thing, or strange change, as well in Civil as Ecclesiastical Government, and when this now Infant Preacht by this starr, shall again visit

---

(*k*) *Alst. Chron.* pag. 493. *Cometography, and some years had 2,3, or 4: in one year since Christ,* Exelius.
(*) *So* Job 38. 33. (*i*) Isa. 13.10. 2 King. 23. 5.
(*l*) *Serarus p.* 21. *at Tannum in* Norroway. p 22.

the Earth, tho, it be a day-ſtar to us, twill burn as a *(m)* furnace on the wicked world.

But I'll conclude now, with that in the Pſalmes, *(n) They alſo that dwell in the uttermoſt parts of the earth, are afraid at thy tokens.*

(m) Pſal. 4. 1, 2. *(n)* Pſal. 65. 8.

The second Sermon, or part.

Matth. 2.2,9,10.

IT is said of one, being in a clear night (but a high winde) at Sea: the Mariners being afraid, he comforted them thus, in the storm; It is impossible we should perish, and have so many eyes (meaning starrs) looking upon us.

By all visible Prognosticks, the whole interest of Christ and his people, seem to be in such a storm, or boding towards it. But look up to heaven, and see how many eyes are there upon us; look into the Firmament; and see what new eyes (*a*) have been set there upon us; look into the world, and behold, what envious and malicious eyes are there upon us, which would certainly plot our ruine. But look into the Church,

---

(*a*) *In a number of Comets, a late years sometimes three in one year, as* 1655.

and behold how many gracious Prophets and good men; how many precious Prayers have a benign *auspicious* aspect toward us; but look last to the Lord, shall we not conclude, it is impossible a people should perish, that have so many eyes, even seven (*b*) eyes, and that from heaven fixt on us?

It is partly from the expectation of evil, and partly from the hope of good aproaching, that I was led to this text. There are divers, and considerable notes have offered themselves already to your observation, the last time, which I may not now repeat.

There is onely one thing (as to my drift and scope) is mainly to be enquired after from this Text; what this star was, or what it meant, which thus appeared unto the wise men?

1. To which, it is answered? according to some Priscillians that supposed it to be the starre of Christ's Nativity or destiny. Now they that do talk of such Doctrine of Nativities, and Destinies from the stars, do speak so much in the dark, that as I think the starr in my text speaks nothing to the purpose, so I am able to Collect no-

---

(*b*) Zach. 3. 9. & 4. 10. & 9. 8.

thing of truth from that anfwer. For fuppofing that (in *Thefi*) to be true, yet (in *Hipothefi*) it 'twill not quadrate nor fuit our Text; for as Chrift was (fure) no ordinary babe, fo nor was this ftarre a common or natural ftarre. There are others that fay, it was a certain divine vertue: This is the expreffion of *Chrofoftome*; but that is a general term: and may be coincident with what follows. And unlefs he means the fourth conjecture (an Angel) I cannot tell what he intends by that divine vertue.

But, thus much may be allowed him (*) there was a certain divine vertue invifible put into this ftar; fo to conduct, and manuduct unto the cradle of Chrift.

There are (again) 3ly. that do fuppofe by it is meant a certain created and newmade ftarre, by a divine hand, fo divers good Authors call it, and it may pafs for fuch a new made ftarre, unlefs we defire to cavil, but,

4thly, There are a fourth fort, that fay it was an Angel.

5thly, There is another, that conjectures it was the Spirit of God.

(*) *Virtutem quandam Invifibilem, feu Angelum in fpecie fyderis figuratum,* Pareus in loc.

But

But becauſe I care not to oppoſe; I would comprehend in my own anſwer, what I ſuppoſe, may not much quarrel with any of theſe expreſſions.

And therefore I anſwer, that it was a certain new-created ſtarre, by the miniſtration, or manuduction of an Angel (if you will) ſet, and ſent on purpoſe for that preſent ſervice, which God appointed it to, for the conducting of theſe wiſe men, convicting of the Jews, and awakening of others; (*) ſo many as ſhould hear on't. And therefore my Queſtion was not onely what it was, but whereto, or for what end? And that is plain and eaſie, 'twas for directing the way of the poor *Arabians*, (as ſome ſay *Perſians*) that in the end they might finde out that *Jeſus*, which was born a King in *Bethlehem*.

And ſo, the knowledge of God, and *Jeſus Chriſt*, and Chriſt's Kingdom (to which he was born) was made known to theſe Aliens, as ſoon, (if not ſooner) then it was to ſome of them Scribes and Rabbies that were in *Jeruſalem*; that yet could tell the place, and very town, (c) where he was to be be born, as *v. 6.*

(*) *One ſayes it was ſent to excite them to preach him at their return; and hence in* Act. 2. 11. *we read of Proſelites of* Arabia. (c) *Bethlehem*, Mic. 5. 2.

Where-

Wherefore *Auſtine* calls it a witneſs of Chriſt; and indeed, it was ſo; though the wiſe men, and the Spirit of God in the Evangeliſt, doe not tell us what the language was; or how they came to a right knowledge of this (that he was a King) yet the thing was a Scripture truth; and we muſt conclude, that all truth hath it's revelation from the God of truth. (*) And this was to convince the Gentiles; therefore *Pareus*, they were the firſt fruits of the Gentiles; theſe that came, (whether they were Kings, two, or three, or more, wiſe men cannot well determine) from ſo remote a place, unto *Judea*: And it was alſo to awaken and convince the heathen-like Jewes, ſo far now degenerate, from the knowledge of God. For by conſulting two or three Doctors, *Hammond, Gell, Mayer*; all theſe three on the Text much agree in the citation of *Chalcidius*, who living about the time of Chriſt, does report the ſacred Hiſtory of this Evangeliſt, and the Report and particular Narrative of this Star, as the old Philoſ. *Chalcid.* is cited part 1 p.

(*) In his *Contemplations*, Biſhop Hall ſayes p. 13. that the light of Nature and of Phyloſophy, taught them that that Starre was not Ordinary, ſome ſtrange news was portended to the world by it.

So

So that by all, we may conclude, that it was a thing created above, and seen in the East, and fixed after in it's particular motion (in a lower Orb) different from all other stars, and new Comets; that it might direct these unto the blessed Babe, and King of the Jews.

From whence I did, and do Observe.

Doctrine, *That when God Creates new Stars, he hath some new and great work to do in the world.*

Whether you'l count me regular in my observation, and right in this Doctrine, by the sequel, your selves shall Judge. But apparent it is, both from the Text and context; That when God Creates certain new Prodigious Stars in the Heavens, or the Air, it must necessarily presignifie, that God is about some new, and great work in the world, either of Judgement or mercy, or both. Which point, will further necessitate us to an enquiry after these four things.

Four Questions,
First, That God doth sometimes Create signal Stars, or Stars for signatures or significations of his minde. There we must a little Demonstrate that it is so. (For if

that same *substratum*, should fall to the ground, all that's built upon it will signifie nothing.)

The Second enquiry will be, what it is these signifie; what new things these are that are likely to be concomitants; (though I say not (†)the effects as of a cause, but) the consequents, or signs, or the attendants of such dreadful (*Phenomena's*) or appearances. And

Thirdly, How, or by what Rule or *norma*, this knowledge must be taken up, or what signatures there are, or mediums, by which such language may be read, either of good, or evil to come?

And there will be a fourth enquiry, which will relate unto the Hypothesis (granting the Thesis, that there are such things) and so discovered, and for such ends; it will be necessary for further light (*& ex abundanti*) to clear from experience (and the knowledge of History in by-past times,) the truth of the thing, that God hath in all Ages almost so done; though *I* dare not say, for every year, but for that defect, sometimes thrice in the year, r, has set up Prodi-

---

(†) Fromund. *non est causa Physica, sed signum mali ad placitum dei; Cometa.*

gious

gious fights, or new ſtarrs in the Heavens, for to preſignifie ſuch events.

But firſt, to the Baſis, (the *quod ſit*,) that this muſt needs be; to which truth, I argue,

Firſt, from the conſideration of the Creator. And the firſt Creation of theſe (ſo called) Starres; Let *Them be for ſigns, and ſeaſons, for dayes and years*, Gen. 1. 14. and the 15. verſe, alſo addes, *for to be lights unto the earth*, or to illuminate and illuſtrate the Earth; which is not ſo much to be underſtood of the bare and meer ſenſitive world, but of the rationalls too, for the night-light of the ſtarres, is but a glimmering light, and inferiour to that of the Moon, excepting ſuch Prodigious ſights, as ſometimes have been in Comets ſeen (*non minor is ſole*) ſuch ſtars have given light, (almoſt like the ſun,) both by their Martial fiery colour and their magnitude, or as big in appearance as the moon, ſuch have been (as Writers ſay,) in ſome Ages by-paſt. For God made the the greater light (the Sun) for day; the leſſer, (the Moon) for night. Therefore the Stars barely in that ſence, did not need to ſupply the light of the Moon, which is the greater; (the leſs ſupplies not the greater.) But by the brightneſs of the old or firſt created, and the ſuperaddition of new (Comet-like) Stars; God might intend (ver. 16, 17) to enlighten the world, and Ages in it, concerning good, or evil coming upon it: And I am not alone (d) in that Exposition. For, there is something in lines, expressely to this sence, in Dr. *Peter Serarius* (a *Holander*) who wrote something of this about the last fiery *Trygon*, on the great conjunction of the Superior Planets in 1665.

Now if you say, this relates to the stars that God made at first; what signifies this to new Stars, which have appeared since? whats this to our Comets.

To this I answer, 'Tis some advantage; for thus I argue, If God appointed the first stars for signs made at the Creation, much more may we conclude that Comets so usually superadded, (as if the first sort too few) do Preach and signifie, that God makes a new thing. As it is said, I'll make a new thing (e) in the Earth. But much more when he makes new things in the Heavens. It is a true rule is given, God (f) (and nature) made nothing in vain. God never set up, either the old, or the new Prodigi-

---

(d) *As* Serarius *pleads in a discourse of conjunctions,* pag. 3, &c. (e) Jer. 31. 22. (f) *Deus & natura nil facit frustra.*

ous Stars, that they might be meer futilous obfervations, ufelefs and empty things for folks to gaze upon, and away; no: For faith one Author, when the Star is gone, yet the thing's not gone; fomething or other of good or evil follows it. (*)

The difficulty of tracing this kind of reading and learning, I hope, (for one Sermon or two) will be fufficient Apology, for my preaching on this fubject; If God fet a Star in Heaven, and makes the Cœleftial fphere a Pulpit for a new thing; it is but meet, we fhould (for once) obferve the Sermon of his works, as well as his word. For, the works of the Lord, (as well Creation, as renewed Creation, which appears in Providence) *are fought out* (g) *of all, that have pleafure therein.*

Secondly, the truth of this figniture further appears, by the verification of old Prophefies hereby, which you fhall finde inftances of as firft that of (†) *Balaam*: There fhall *come a ftarre out of* Jacob, *and a Scepter fhall rife out of Ifrael* (the Scepter is an Emblem of Dominion) (The Starre

---

(*) *Nullus Cometes qui nullum malum ferat.*
(g) Pfal. 111. 2. (†) For that fome do recite *Maldonat. Paræus* notes *Probabile divinitus oraculo admonitos, & Inftinctu divino, licet hoc taceant.*

then, signified Dominion, as you finde it in the 24 of *Numbers*, the 17 verse). and shall smite the Corners of *Moab*, and unwall (as *Ainsworth* reads it) all the children of *Seth*, which, though I will not be peremptory to say, he solely meant this star which was attendant to the Nativity of our Lord; (*) yet because out of the line of *Jacob* came this blessed babe, who was to be the King of the *Jews*, and the redeemer of the world; it must imply certainly, thus much, that *Balaam* had an eye in his Prophesie to this: or God, in delivering this Prophesie to him, and by him to us. Nor do *I* think that Prediction all; For if you please to consult a verse or two in the 72 *Psalm*; which is a Psalm of Christ, under the type of *Solomon*, you shall finde this very thing and place indigitate, and the circumstances and concomitants of it, therefore must needs be implyed. The 72 Psalm 10, and the 15 verse. *The Kings of Tarshish, and of the Isles shall bring Presents: the Kings of Sheba, and Seba, shall offer gifts.* One of these places must be this East country, whence these came; as learned Authors think. Again it is used in the 15. verse.

(*) *Bishop* Hall *saith, he that put that true Prophesie into* Baalams *mouth, put his own Illumination in their hearts,* Cont. pag. 14.

think.

And he shall live (not an infant born meerly to dye; though he dyed, he lives for evermore,) *and to him shall be given of the gold of Sheba*: (for mark; they brought gold, frankincense, and myrrhe) all belonging to that East Countrey.

2. Yet there is a Prophesie more, that may be adduced to this, *viz.* in the 60 of *Isaiah*: (and that's a great Prophesie of the glory of the Church, her King, and Kingdom. (For the Church is Christ's Kingdom, and he is her King) the glory of this Church is much exprest in this 60 of *Isaiah*, saith the 6 verse, *The multitude of Camels shall cover thee, the Dromedaries of Midian and Ephah, all they from Sheba shall come: they shall bring gold and incense, and they shall shew forth the praises of the Lord.* These are plain and palpable Prophesies) and could no otherwise nor better be verified, then herein. Now from one of these places, *Sheba* and *Seba*, It is said, the Queen of *Sheba* came from the South. (So called the Queen of the South) Therefore the other place *Seba*, must be from the East. And so here are the several parts, round about *Jerusalem* nam'd; for that was supposed the Navel of the earth. Here Christ Jesus was pleased to discover himself in our flesh; here he is saluted by the Shepherds

in the field; by the Prophets of the old Testament; by the Angels from Heaven; by the wise men Eastward; Some will needs call them Kings from the East. But that Jesuitical Tradition, is deservedly exploded that when these (*h*) three they say wise Kings had returned to their own countrey; they were from their Sepulchers translated and buryed at *Cullen* (*i*) by Queen *Merome*. But this was onely designed to feed the Coffers of those that were superstitiously affected. Now I say, that Prophesie, which does respect the whole, respects all the other circumstances and parts of things.

If then you ask what these speak? they are Prophesies of the wise men; what should conduct them? or who? either,

1. Some, Prophet of *Israel*, but that is not said at all;

2. Or else they knew from some Trade, & commerce the Merchants of the Jews, had among them, for incense, myrrhe, &c. which is not exprest at all, tho probable, or,

---

(h) *But to say they were three, not more or less, or Kings of* Cullen *is a fancy as futilous as the legend of Popish fictions.* (i) *And some do presume to name the three Kings, the first* Jasper, *the second* Melchior, *the third* Balthasar, *and some use them as a spell to cure the Fallen-sickness, and conclude as once I saw and read it.* Solvitur à morbo domini pietate caduco.

3. Lastly,

3. Laftly, By the directions and oracular dictates that attended this Star : and the Lord by fome inftinct, divinely revealing it to them, for the ufual way of God was, and is, to fecond weak and outward means with the more inward, and effectual revelation of the Spirit, (of which by and by.)

Now I fay, when there are Scripture-predictions, that (in General) fpeak of it in the old Teftament, and the new Teftament reports the verification in our Text, then it muft needs be a truth,(and *Luk.* 21.25. alfo attefts it) that God makes and frames fuch figns, on purpofe, and ftill Chrift predicts it of our dayes : for fome great work he hath to do ; thus it is verified by Prophefie, as well as Creation.

3. And for the third. I argue from the experience of thefe wife men. For fhall we think that they were deluded ? that they were conducted by fuch an heavenly apparition ; to come, they know not whether, nor for what end ? no doubtlefs, all the circumftances that did attend, from all this whole revelation, do fpeak the truth by their experience of the thing. And what the Scriprure fpeaks before was their experience, and fo had need to be owned for truth. Therefore 'twas certainly a fign Cœleftial manuducting them to Chrift ;

for

for they being true to its conduct by that ſtar found Chriſt. For in the circumſtances of the Text, its clear their evidence and experience fail'd them not.

Firſt of all, you finde, that ſo ſoon as he was born: (and ſome do ſuppoſe, within the mothers moneth, before he was preſented at *Jeruſalem*) they took their Journey: which ſome conjecture (*l*) was on foot; Others, by thoſe ſwift beaſts which thoſe Countreys afforded. I ſay, I affirm nothing in that; But ſo many dayes they might have, (at the rate of thirty or forty miles a day,) to bring them unto *Bethlehem* before her moneth was out. But however, this is certainly affirmed, the Star is ſaid to appear twice. 1. It appeared firſt in their own Countrey; for we have ſeen his Star in the Eaſt. Yet again (a ſecond time the Star did appear, when they had ſlipt it: or it was lapſed out of ſight from them, or rather I think they gone aſide from it, and thinking that the Metropolis of a Kingdom was the likelyeſt way to diſcover where a King was born; however they loſt the conduct of the Star, when they went to *Jeruſalem*;

(*l*) *Others ſay, 'twas above a twelve moneth,* Mary *being return'd to a ſecond Tax to that Town.*

which was not the straitest, and nearest way to *Bethlehem* (one thinks) but about, distant seven or eight miles from *Jerusalem*. And when they came out from *Jerusalem* again, the Star appeared the second time, *and they were exceeding glad*, so saith the context, at the 9, & 10, verses. Yet more-over *Herod* himself seems to (*m*) be troubled, or affrighted, at the rumour, as in a storm) Plannet-struck with the tydings of a new king born. For he being an *Edomite*, (and as one truly sayes; every thing affrights the guilty) a very wicked man, a destroyer of his wives, a murtherer of his children, and of all those that thought, or were intended for the Succession, an enemy to the Countrey, (*) and the Sanedrim or Senators of the Jews, to God and Religion; of the *Amalekitish*, or *Edomitish* stock; This Hypocrite to Christ, is mightily amazed and amused at the report of such a thing "And *Herod*, (saith the third verse) hearing of it, and all *Jerusalem*, was greatly concern'd, or amuzed. For it doth greatly concern the Potentates of this world, when they hear

---

(*m*) ἐταράχθη, at ver. 3. *as the Sea waves that swell, and boyl up their rage, and foul mudd.* (*) *Josephus sayes, he sought to destroy them all nigh his end.*

of

of a Governour born, or right-heir that is like to succeed them, better then themselves. It is the observation of one, (*n*) Tyranny is still suspitious of a rival) that not onely he but all *Jerusalem* (the Text saith) were troubled at him. Whether it was because they had a King already: and they had no mind nor care to hear of another; or it was because they were so much in love with him, (as bad as he was) that they thought the next would be worse, and therefore they were very desirous to feed him with Hypocrisie, flattery, or whatever 'twas, it is said, he, and all *Jerusalem* were mightily jumbled with the tydings, that they were affrighted to think of a change: which, had they with the Magi, but seen such a Star, or consider'd the Text in *Micah*, 5.2.ver.6.8. and the Prophesies of him, it would not at all have amused them.

And besides the Text saith, it was called his Star; *we have seen his Star*. And when they saw the Star again, v. 2, 9. they

---

(*n*) *Bishop* Halls *contempl. on the Magi. So had this City been overtoyled with changes, that (now settled in a condition quietly evil,) they're sore troubled at all the news of better: and so inured to servility, that the noyse of liberty (that comes uneasily) is unwelcome*, pag. 15.

were exceeding glad, all show it in the thing it self, and its end too! extraordinary. And that shews the last Circumstance; Being wise men, they would not rejoyce for nothing.

All these things put together, make the several Circumstances clear enough, for the truth of the thing observ'd, (*viz.*) that this Star was a great, a certain, and most visible sign, both to lead them to Chrifts Nativity at present, and that God for the future had some extraordinary product to entertain the eyes of the now expectant World with good or evil.

To all this, may be added, that in the days of *Augustus*, there was a certain sign of a Virgin in the Heavens, appearing over *Rome*, with a Babe in her Lap; and somewhere * read—(If we may believe Antient stories, the Emperour being much concerned, about Chrifts Nativity sent to a *Sybil* (some call her a Witch:) what she

---

* *Another Cites* Sybil. Cumana. Last. *and others.* Syb. Erythrea or Caldaica, *that all do speak of Chrifts incarnation.*

was

was, I know not.) But this she said unto him,

This Child's thy greater, him therefore,
Thou art commanded to adore.

    This sign was also co-incident about this time, and it is further evident, that not only *Jerusalem* and all *Judea*, but even the World about, (for they all went under the *Romans* at this time) had special cognizance or previous sentiments of some great thing that was now to be brought forth into the World. That's for the First.

    The second thing will be brief, only to answer what these new Signs signifie.

    And as to this I have almost prevented my self already; telling you that they are signs, sometimes of one thing, sometimes of another quite contrary. But I'le tell you in particular a Little.

    First, As the Old, so also the New. Comets (and Stars) that appear in the Heavens, they are signs of the great Wisdom of God.

    For certainly in Wisdom (*Ps.* 104. 24.) he made them all. They have a glorious signature, though it is not easie to read every line; yet we read that their line & Language is gon to the end of the World. *Ps.* 19 4.

What

What do the Stars preach of? (we can tell what we do, euery day, to litle purpose.) What do the Stars Preach of? The Heavens declare the Glory of God, and the Firmament sheweth his handy work. And how is the handy work made to testifie of him? Truly, Had one nothing but the Laws of Astronomy, it must needs signifie by what is seen, the eternal, invisible Gods skill, or to read over the Motions, Conjunctions, Configurations, and several aspects and retrogradations, which are to be observed: and by the meer Law of the Heavens somewhat of God is cognoscible, which *Abraham* knew; * and *Job* and *Moses* also: and therefore that lawful Art of Astronomy must needs read to the attentive observer abundance of the Wisdom of God beside his power, veracity, *&c.* in the least work he makes, in Heaven, and Earth. But they,

2dly. They signifie the displeasure of God often show'd against Sin; and so are sometimes black lines and signs of Evil, boding upon the sinful Sons of men, and call even the utmost parts of the Earth to fear Gods

---

* *God ratifies his Covenant to Abraham by setting him to contemplate the Stars.* Gen. 15. 5. *it was done in the night.*

Tokens

Tokens as *Pf.* 65. 8. Every Tranfgreffion hath its reward decreed, and judgments delineated in Heaven. But fometimes God hath patience with the Sons of men, and will tarry a great time, *Gen.* 6. 3. (as 120 years warning the World) and fets them up a Preacher to tell them, by ocular Mathematical demonftration; well, this fhews you, there's a dreadful tail of arrears to pay, a long rod over your heads: thus they are figns of the Wrath of God. They are,

Thirdly, Signs of Chrift; though I do not fay, in this, or that way: (that's yet to enquire) but certainly, this Scripture which I am upon doth fpeak fignificantly this Language, That the Star did preach Chrift, elfe why is the Query backt with the caufall particular. For? All the Queftion is, How thefe wife men of the *Eaft* fhould come to read fo Divine Language of Chrifts coming and being a King, in the Laws of the natural Motions in general, or fupernatural appearance of this Star in particular? Unto which I only fay in a few words, yet more exprefs.—(for the mediums or rules I referve to the 3. Q.

Firft, That God had a minde (certainly) that Chrift fhould be revealed (in his Gofpel and Kingdom, and that at firft:) as well

to

to the Gentiles, as the Jews (in the way proper and apt to both) and about the same time, that he was first born, that so he might be a Saviour, as well to Gentiles, as Jewes; that so, these poor sinners might obtain, (as well as the Jewes did) the first of his Doctrine, and benefits:

(omnes Quum gentes Christum agnoscunt generaliter, Ultima Evangelium, legem quæ prima recepit. Quos docuit primos, postremos Christus habebit.

(Grace,
When once the Gentiles all are drawn to
Then will the Jews the Gospel truth embrace:
Who first the Law, last shall the Gospel have:
Christ whom he first did call, shall last receive.

Is a saying very florid, of *Peter Domianus*, that the Jewes, that were first taught the Law, should be the last converted to the Gospel, and the Gentiles should be as the first fruits after their fall: and then should all the Jewes come in too; and so it should be glory and riches to the whole world.

And I say yet further, That they are also sometimes Nuncio's of wrath, and otherwhile

while the more rarely signs of (*) good: You know sin is more frequent (and finds more friends) in the world, then Piety and goodness, that obtain but with a few) and therefore wrath and Judgement, must not be wondred at, if found louder in its alarums; then the Graces and Vertues of a few poor, tho precious ones in the world, and Appearances of wrath suited to those vices that are, in the latter times, are far more frequent then appearances of Grace; though there are better dayes Prophesied of, saith (p) *Virgil*, citing one of the *Sybiles*

Ultima Cumæi venit jam carminis ætas,
Magnus ab Integro seclorum nascitur ordo,
Jam redit & virgo; Redeunt Saturnia regna.

Now (saith he) shall the Virgin come, and now shall return those glorious golden dayes: for so they supposed the *Saturnian* times to be.

So that my answer (in short, to the second question) may amount to this, what one Author somewhere did observe from one of the *Sybiles*; it is said, that

---

(*) David prayes in Psal. 85. 17. For a token of good; that notes, such there are, as well as of evil. (p) 4 Ecclog. cited by a late Authour.

upon

upon the appearance of this Star, there was a new Doctrine, a new King, and Kingdom of Chriſtianity to riſe in the World: And it was very true, and very well gueſt; for from the days of Chriſt, during all the preaching of his own miracles; all the Doctrines of his Apoſtles for threeſcore years following his Death: and ſo (all along) during the time of Martyrdom; What indefatigable endeavours have been to root up both the Doctrine and Authority too of Chriſtianity; but it could never be done, no, nor I hope, never, never will.

Therefore when ſuch things ariſe, they are Phenomena's or certain appearances; and prodigious diſcoveries: Indicia's, or ſignifications oft-times of evil, and alſo of great good that will follow afterwards in the world.

To come to my third Enquiry (for particular Inſtances: I am not yet come to, or to the practick part.)

It is Thirdly to be conſidered by what mediums, or what norma's be they, (if they be Prognoſticks,) by which theſe ſignatures in the Stars, or in this Star, in ſpecial

cial must be read, or understood?

If a thing may be known, then the mediums, by which it becomes intelligible, must needs be also Indigitated and discoverable. Now here in the General, the Answers are many; and those that have a Mind to pick out the best, must choose where they like best.

Conjectures may be honest, but Conclusions are of more use if certain and clear.

How may the Signatures of Gods mind, in Creation of the stars and Comets be known?

There's some answers doubtful or sinful, some lawful, but not pertinent: and some are probable Conjectures: I'le labour (in that I say) to remove the weaker, and conclude and clear the likelier Opinions that carry strength of Reason, and Scripture in them.

1. There are, that say, It is by a certain innate Law, which God the first cause gives the Planets and Comets over mens Nativities or genitures, and by the lines of Chrifts Nativity

Nativity) the *Magi* calculated their Inquiry. But where that Law is written, and what the Law and Language of it is, they are not able to report, and besides the Star did not govern Christ (tho' it testified of him:) but he it.

2. There are others (again) that conclude hence the necessity and utility of Judicial Astrology, and the lawfulness of it, and that the wise men by this art, in a Scheam (or Ephemeris) of the Planets, knew Christ to be King. But because I find in the Scripture so much of Gods reprehension and reproach put upon these things and the practisers thereof; and sometimes Sentences of Death due unto these by the Laws and Statutes of men; I dare, in no wise plead the lawfulness of that art. For see the 47 of *Isaiah* 12, 13. *Let now the Astrologers, the Star-gazers, the Monthly Prognosticators stand up and save thee from those things that shall come upon thee.* (r) God made the Heavens black and dark over them, or made their lines illegible, or made his hand undiscoverable; his Judgment upon *Babylon*, was not to be investi-

---

(r) *For being set in Conjunction with Inthantments, and both under Gods reproof it follows the Star-gazers were wicked, and their Sin was Capital, yea, and the judgment Astrological, futulous and false.*

gated

gated by that art, there was no footsteps left in the cœlestial Planetary course that justly could Prognosticate her ruin.

Calvin (s) does observe upon that Text thus much, (which is to my purpose) that the Lords mind and purpose was to leave the Judgment of *Babylon* without any foretoken, or presignature, any way, either in the Stars, or otherwise; that it might be known to be the sole hand and peculiar (hidden) finger of God, and his own sentence upon *Babylon*; she should know by no Star, nor no means, or permonition how she should fall. (t) And though it is true, that *Daniel* is called the Master of the Magicians; yet we are to distinguish, (as part the first before,) for there is a great difference between that Diabolical Magick, which they now study and plead for, in an Astrological way; and that holy, and heavenly Wisdom that *Daniel* studyed and perhaps some (from him or his Scholers,) learned by the knowledge of the Law and will of God. And though he was by the

---

(s) *Exitium quod Cald. Imminebat previdere non potuerunt, ut pote quod ex naturali astrorum cursu non emanavit, sed ex arcano Dei concilio.* (t) *And if not the fall of* Babylon, *is calculate by Astrology, how could the Magi collect the rise, or the regality of Christ by it, without a special Revelation.*

Queen

Queen call'd Master of the Magicians *Dan.* 4. 9. ch. 5. 11. not his own Title but theirs; and so might be an instrument to save some of their lives, (not a Dr. of their Diabolick art) that they might believe in his God and learn at his prophetick oracle, not their own, and repent of their wicked art; (For, Sinners are not immediately to be cut off.) All this style given *Daniel*, doth not speak the lawfulness of that Diabolical Magick art at all. *Perkins* (and other holy Writers also) refute the arguments adduced, for judicial Astrology. *Pareus* p. 614 shews how futelous, and untrue their arguments are that seek from their judicial Astrology, and arguments from the Stars, to discover Christ. (*v*)

3. There are (again,) Thirdly, Those that do conjecture more tollerably; that the discovery of the Divine will, by a Star or new Comet, is to be took out from the several Conjunctions, which usually do precede such Comets appearances; Now of the eight Conjunctions, which they say, the Stars have had in the Coelestial World:

(*v*) *Let Sir* C. H. *Dr.* G. Will. Lilly, Booker, *and Scurrilous* W. *and now* J. Gad. *plead in favour of it at pleasure, 'tis out of my way to stay in that puddle.*

(taking

(taking in the firſt; which was juſt at the Creation a little before the fall:) there have alwayes, or for the moſt part, within a year or two, been very great and wonderful prodigious appearances in the Heavens, the Air, Earth (*v*) and Waters too; on which changes have been ſeen in Empires; and ſo by the Language of thoſe (*w*) conjunctions and configurations of the Stars; ſuch dictates muſt be diſcovered. But this I leave to thoſe that are ſtudious in that Aſtronomical Art; it is not ſo proper for a Religious and Theological diſcourſe, and for plain vulgar Capacities. I confeſs, that Reverend Dr. *Gell*, once preaching to the Society of this kind of Students of *Greſham-Colledge*, here in this City, not many years ago, doth ſeem to ſpeak ſomething favourable of Aſtrology in his *Stella nova*: *Anno* 49. *pag.* 2. 6, *and* 9. But becauſe he is dead and gone, I will let his judgment alone, and not impeach his deſerved gravity, parts, and piety with a word.

4. There are others from the ſigna-

(*v*) *As the Poets ſay, putrique cruore mutati.* (*w*) *The Opinion of Dr.* P. Serarius *(a very pious and Learned* Hollander, *in a diſcourſe on the laſt Conjunction in* Sagitary, *in* Decemb. Anno 62. *followed with three Comets in* Decemb. 64. *in which he predicts the Kingdom of Jeſus Chriſt at hand.*

tures

tures of the Comets themselves, their site, course, colours or kinds; For when a Comet appears that is fiery and brisk, (*) then, say they, it imports War; when a Comet appears that is dark and leaden, and of a *Saturnian* colour, and with a long Tail, that portends diseases, dissentions, deaths, Plagues, and oft Seditions: and cite *Haly*, *Kep'er*, *Tycho Brahe*, and them I wave. I remember *Hen. Alstede* treats in his peculiar Cometographical History of two Hundred and sixty Comets, and enumerates about 31 other Authors. He tells you of some that had appeared, *caudâ ablongâ*, with a very long Tail, much like this, whose Tail has yet it's remains: Very long in the Heavens, but of a mighty envious colour, and Ominous portent: and this is the longest (save one) that I read of; which in its effects portends as (I said) the product of mortality, as in the sequel will be after particulariz'd. At present (in general) I often find, after one Comet a dreadful sweating sickness in *England*, that swept Millions of the *English* (and them only) away, travelling any where. After another Comet a dreadful Pestilence

---

* *This way go most of our Philosophers and Naturalists of late.*

raged

raged almost through the whole World, *pestis per totum mundum grassatur. pag.* 492. *Annis* 1500, and 1527. (saith my Author,) Now these first Stars, or new Comets are not mute dumb Prophets when they come to speak such kind of Language, as collating the former, with our late Comet they plainly do.

There's one Rule more, and that's this, judge wisely by the help of former Ages, Sins, signs, and measure of events.

5. By Experience. There is no man that observes well what he reads, and what he sees; what he reads in his own Books, what he observes in Gods book, Nature, or Scripture, in the Heavens, and in the works and courses of men upon earth; but by colating and comparing the sins of men, with Gods fury, but will conjecture, (x) nay may certainly conclude by experience, that some great thing, (of good perhaps to few) likely of evil to many; is boding upon the world, and impending over it.

Here now, it were easie, to compare the former Stars, which have been proposed to the worlds view (*) since the memory of 1572, and that *Parisian* Massacre. The Star in the Chayre (so call'd) of *Cassiopeia*;

(x) Alsted. * *If these be to be counted Comets.*

also

also that following it, in 1618, a most brisk and clear martial one. One Collonel *Fenwick* having been in *Germany*, sees it there; coming over the water in the *Thames*, sees it there; The colour, and it's motion, strange, and dreadful, its streams-fiery: and as doleful things following it. Now reckon but by that *An.* 1665. Three in that one year did appear, (we felt the events) It hath been rare, saith my Author, for a Comet to have been seen in an age; There have been five in an hundred years: sometimes ten in one Age, and three now in one year. And by comparing with it the consequences thereof, recollect after the year 1664, and that dusky gloomy Comet in *December*, what a dreadful Pestilence ensu'd in 1665, to omit the other signs of wrath succeeding, and all other Prodigies that were since.

Why then, one may calculate and gather, there's nothing (by the rule of experience) that hath been, (as *Solomon* said, *Eccles.* 1. 9, 10.) but may be again.

One Authour speaks of twelve sorts of Comets, of them some like Lances, some like Swords, a third sort like Spits, or darts: some as beards, brushes or long rods. There is one most Terrible, that hath a long brush, these speak the most fatal things in their own Characters, and Colours

lours.) I will not gather conclusions to terrifie you altogether: but thus much I may conjecture safely, That by such Mediums, and signatures, the Characters of Prodigious signs may be decypher'd, and somewhat of God and Christ read by them. I may superadde because a learned Author, (Dr. *Burthogg*) is pleased to say thus much, (which may serve for a Sixth answer.)

6 *Rule*. God sometimes sixthly makes out to poor dark Heathens his minde by over-ruling Diabolicall Enthusiasms and conjurers, (as *Balaam*,) to speak his mind to some, in things future, truly, For, which of you will doubt (to speak from Scripture now,) (*) in *Numb*. 24. 17.) you may see the History of *Balaam*, no body denyes Mr. *Atterfol*'s opinion, that he was a very hellish Conjurer, a very wicked man: (the onely Jesuit plotting, with *Balaac*, *Israels* ruine) And yet, who shall doubt of the truth of that Prophesie, (of the Messiah) in the figure of the glorious Star of *Jacob*, to whom the Scepter belongs.

(*) So *Laban* sayes unto *Jacob* in Gen. 20. 27. I learn'd by experience (*in the Hebrew Diviration*) who it seems owns the Integrity of *Jacob*.

Here's

Here's a man a Devilish Seer, and yet had a most Divine Vision, and guided by a Diabolical Art, and Spirit, but over-rul'd by temporary Impellings of God's Spirit.

The Age is sometimes so wicked, that not onely God himself doth preach it, but hee'l make the Devil himself to preach, So Satan (under *Samuels* mantle) prov'd *Sauls* Chaplin, and preach't such dreadful Language, that better he had never consulted his fortune at that she Oracle.

Well, to give one other instance besides this, see too in the Margin (†) *Saul* goes to hell to consult: *And wherefore hast thou raised me up*, saith the Devil? (speaking in the person of *Samuel*?) Why (saith he) God is departed from me, and I am sore distressed, v.15. troubl'd v.21. Mark it, what a dreadful Doctrine did the Devils spectrum preach to him? All most terrible news, (for it indeed stund him.) And it is the the hardest thing (almost) to strike terror into Kings that so terrifie others.

Saul, a man of such valour and resolution, 1 *Sam.* 28. all the end of that Chapter

---

(†) *That witch was Sauls Gypsie, or Sybil, and Caiaphas was guided by their light, Jo.*11.51. *God so over-ruling him.*

for this fee more writ of the Oracles and the Sybils. in that Learned Dr. *Burthogg, de caufa dei, ad fin: p.* 350, 360, 370.

And yet (faith the Text) he fainted away, when told to morrow, thou and thy Sons fhall be with me. And it is ufual, and juft with the Lord, when wicked men leave the will of God, and go to the way of the Devil; that the Devil fhould preach dreadful Doctrine to them; and fo he did to *Saul*.

I'le only fuper-add one thing more, and fo let this difquifition fall.

So Seventhly and Laftly, The *Magi* furely had by and with that Star, the internal Oracle, and Revelation of the Spirit; fo that whatfoever other wayes, to other Perfons might be ufed, this was laft and is beft Guide unto Jefus. Nor could any of the fix firft be effectual, had the Lord denyed this. Thus you fee they that follow Divine leading (tho' their light be lefs) fhall furely be conducted to the Lord Jefus at laft; whilft their falfe and furious adverfaries are difappointed, and fhall be (in due time) feverely plagued of God; and

difdispatcht as this Tyrant (*Herod*) was, by Death: and so the Issue of the Star was Jesus safe Exile, a blessed return to *Joseph* and *Mary*, and also the exordium of that Kingdom of Christ took place under the Cross, that shall have no end.

The Third Sermon, or part.

Matth. 2. 2, 9, 10.

IN the 145 *Psalm.* 6. 7. Compared with the 10, 11, 12. verses; you will (among other things) Observe these two Notes: as introductory to the sequel intended.

First, That memorable and wonderful works, and the Kingdom of God, usually concur. When God is about to exalt his Son Christ to propagate, and revive the Glory of his Kingdom, he doth it by precedaneous prodigies and wonderful works. These works of God go before: the Kingdom and King himself do follow after: (as at Solemn Coronations.) And

Secondly, That it is the duty of all especially *Saints*) greatly to observe, and to utter one to another; yea, and to convey down to following Generations, the memory of Gods works, and the Glory of his Kingdom, one Generation shall utter to another (abundantly) the Glory thereof.

What *Matthew* the Evangelist (and he only) observed in his time, is here conveyed down to us. What efforts of God's Kingdom are observable in our time, should be by History Chronicled and Conveyed down, unto the following generation. The little significancy (God knows) that the Word of God (for so long time) hath had among us; hath made me to set my Pulpit (as it were) a little higher, and look into the Cœlestial works of God; of which, that late Star, (now expired) was, and is so memorable, and so significant, to see if that kind of Preaching may also serve to testifie and awaken.

The History of Christ you see, in the infancy of his Kingdom, is here, by the Evangelist notified, by certain wonderful and strange things concomitant; and none of them more, then this particular Star (in our Text,) the only new Comet, (if I may so call it) or strange Star, that we read of, in al the two Testaments, Old, and New. And the Point (among many others that I only glanc'd at,) which I have chosen out for this present subject was,

That

That God sometimes signifieth much of his mind concerning good or evil to come, by the signature of his works, and parcularly of new Stars in the Heavens.

I confess, the word is his ordinary medium or method of dealing with his People, (and was among the *Jews*:) (*a*) others must, by signs ordinary, or extraordinary be taught; but the works of God sometimes do open a wide mouth to speak for him to both; so did this star.

I have laboured to resolve three questions already. And now pass to the fourth Question.

As for our third Question, How this Language is uttered, or how it may be learned? I only say, there are unlawful studies, and irregular Rules; which neither have the word for Scripture Philosophy; (and all other is vain Phylosophy,)(*b*) nor yet any right reason in nature to ground it: And therefore by these, nothing certain can be known. It must therefore either be by the form and Characters; or that course and Method of those Stars, or Comets. As to instance in this new, it was

---

(*a*) *Ps.* 147, 19, 20. (*b*) *Col.* 2. 8. ϰỳ ϰενῆς ἀπάτης.

F 2

a peculiar new created thing, in its motion, not in the upper Sphere; but in the lower Region of the air, in its paffage, not fo fwift as other Planets above be.

But according as thefe wife men could move in that long Journey, to find Chrift. Laftly its fite, or fcituation: was in the lower part of the air, for the pointing out, and indigitating of the houfe; which it could not have done, if it had not been very low.

Alfo this fignification is given more inwardly by Oracle as well as occularly; And this, either by the ftudying of the Art Aftronomical, and Laws of the Planets, which is a lawful thing, or elfe by a Divine (fhall I call it, a Scripture) Magick or Wifdom, for there is fuch a thing lawful, (like that of *Mofes*, and *Daniel* that is a Wifdom Divine,) not what is now accounted Diabolical; or by fome wonderful Angels fent down on purpofe to preach this for the fign of Chrifts Kingdom. This is the work you fhall do, to Jewry is the Journey you muft take; and there at *Bethlehem* certainly you fhall find the Redeemer. Therefore fome Authors fay, it was an Angel. I would rather fay it was an Angel, conducting both it and them. And others as truly conclude, it was by the peculiar

liar motion of the Spirit of God; † which (together with the outward teaching of the Heavens) gave them an inward teaching and instruction from above. This is the sign, this is the thing signified; go so far, and there you shall see the glorious King of the *Jews*, in the Embrio of his Kingdom. And by consulting one passage, a little after, in the same Chapter; it is said, in a verse or two below, that when they would have gone to *Herod*, there were warned of God: † χρηματισθέντες. (saith the *Greek*) being Oracularly, or by a voice from Heaven warned. Now I say, if God by a miraculous escape, would give them an Oracular voice to preserve them from *Herods* craft and fury, to save natural life: much more may we think for their Souls eternal good, by the Oracular voice of the Spirit of God, were these poor Creatures conducted eleven hundred and odd miles, from *Arabia Felix*, unto this place where Christ was. (c.)

Fourthly and Lastly; I stood engaged, (and am your Debtor) in yet one more En-

---

† *The same that the Shepherds there had, so the Magi and Shepherds are wiser then the Scribes and Priests. Surgunt indocti, & rapiunt cœlum.* † v. 12. *Divinitus dictum us'd. Act.* 11. 26. *also* Hebr. 11. 7. *so the Christian name took its* Origine *and Noahs safety from the Flood.* (c) *Reciting the* 3 *heads is a fairer transition to the* 4*th.*

quiry: And that is relating to the Hypothesis, granting the thing (in thesi,) that there is such warnings given, such significations by such miraculous Stars, and an heavenly voice in them; by which, something of good, or evil may be known; which if the Authority of this Scripture had not shew'd me; I had never spoke so long upon this Subject: It will be meet then, I should insist further upon the Induction or Examples of the thing; that the Truth may appear by some one, or more instances.

That as it was with these wise men, that were truly guided to the Babe or King of Glory at's first coming, so most certainly, God hath wonderfully in all ages brought forth some great and evident Tokens of his Kingdom and second coming: partly in his judicial proceedings, inflicting of evil (in our latter times especially;) and partly in those *meliora speranda* (as one saith;) those hoped for good things, that were, and yet are to follow.

Now that which I do affirm in the Hypothesis, is this,

That

That when God is about some great work, that he hath to bring forth in the World; for a Preface to't, he hath in all ages (by past, yet doth and will!) set some memorable signs or portents in the Heavens.

Jeremy the 32. and the 20. verse doth take notice of it, as to the fact: which hast set signs and wonders in the Land of *Egypt*, even unto this day, and in *Israel*, and amongst (d) other men, (or in *Adam*, saith he; so the *Hebr.* (d) So that *Heathens*) as well as *Jews*, might be observers. Christ himself will also confirm the Prophet; For saith he, (speaking of the last times,) in the 21 *Luk.* 25 verse. *And there shall be signs in the Sun and in the Moon and in the Stars.* How in the Stars? Either it may be interpreted of the Stars that are already made. Or in, is as much, as among the Stars, that God himself would appear Gloriously, in making and working new things, and in creating new Star-like Comets; that so it might appear both by the old and the new Stars; that there is some great thing (by the signs) signified. For so,

---

(d) בְּאָדָם (d) *in* Hebr. מִצְרַיִם (i.e.) *portenta posuisti in Israel ubi adam* (i.) *in reliquis hominibus*

elsewhere, (in, is among) *Luk.* 17.21. *The Kingdom of God is within you,* (we read it;) but the Greek elsewhere bears it as well, (*Rom.* 1. 19. & 16. 7.) is among you, so for signs, in the Stars, that is, among the Stars of the Heavens, that is in Comets as well as reall Stars.

Now, because I rather study your profit, then curiosity;(for that was never my intent, to solemnize an act of worship, to please curiosity;) There are two things that will make out this last branch of enquiry in both parts.

1. That new sights, or signs in the Heavens, do precede and presage some dreadfull evil; And

2. Of great good, they are nuncios,

I find, That there are instances in Ages by-past of both sorts: If you say, can they be signal of good, and bad? two contra's. I answer, yea, respecting different objects, persons, and places: as the Protestants and Papists; the Godly and ungodly: Now that that presages all good to the Godly notes evil to the world, (*& vice versa*) so portents on *Egypt,* had signs of good to *Israel.* So *Isa.* 3. 10. & 21, 12. a morning and a night, may at one and the same time, come to differing Interests, and persons,

sons, and some within our own memory, of the truth of this And both these being a little touched upon, (and no more than is needfull;) 'twill sufficiently open a way for more practical doctrine, by way of use. And

First, I say, That the great signs in the heavens are portents of evil; and that usually, when some more then ordinary evil of sin is perpetrated in the world; there are some more then ordinary significators placed above, to those that are (like these wise men) dilligent observers, and fit to read them.

As for that indeed, which is a more large subject, the sad and dismal effects or (if you will) efforts, or consequences of great sins. There is scarce a Judgement you can name, that ever hath been in the world, to punish offences; but God hath made some sign in the Heaven thereof, and some particular Comet, or new Star, the preacher on't; (or, as one calls it) the Nuncio, and witness to it. See some Instances. A little then, to instance, first are most dreadful and terrible overturning winds, and Whirl-winds; sad instances of evil inflicted upon the World. (*) overturning 600 houses, burning whole

---

(*) *High winds Hericano's In the time of* W. Rufus *towards the end of his raign; as* Speed, p. 448.

woods

woods, storms like Hericanoes. I have observed in my reading of times past oft such things; and in our own Chronicles, such things may be read.

About that time a great Comet, two brushes (f) appeared some say 11 or 1200 years ago, there was a dreadful Hericano-wind fell upon this City. And saith *Speed*, (who is grave and sober, and speaks as Religiously, as most of our Chroniclers) did so overturn this place here in *London*, called *Bow-Church*, (now a new thing) that the beams on the top, was taken up into the Air, then thrown into the street (then unpayed) and sunk 23 foot into the ground; such were the consequents of that Comet; about 1100 years.

2. Do we think Inundations of waters to be a dreadful and sore judgement? Indeed it is so. (To say nothing of other Political changes and mutations) in the course of the Tyde, († in the Sea. We read in the History of *Saxony*, *Anno*. 912. some hundred

---

(f) *The Stars seem'd to shoot darts at one another: and by a dart Rufus after was slain by* W. Tirrell. *Earl Goodwins Land, turn'd to Goodwins Sands.*

(†) *A conjunction in the time of* Noah, *precedes that deluge.*

years

years ago; That there was a great Inundation, which deſtroyed, both many places and Villages, and ſome thouſands of people, 40000 *Anno* 1569; alſo by an innudation of water, (*g*) which followed in *Holland* upon another Star, that a little before appeared, and Cardinal *Woolſey* dyes, the *Turks* take *Buda* in *Hungary*.

3. Do we think ſcarcity of fruits, drying up of the Earth, want of food (*annona caritas*) to be a dreadful and ſore Judgement? (*) a Judgement, that we have yet not much experience of in *England*, But God knows what by the dark language of this Star we may do. It is eaſie to produce at leaſt a dozen inſtances of great Comets which have appeared; as *Anno* 1500, *peſtis & fames graſſantur*, and have immediately, (within a year) been attended with ſuch ſad Peſtilence and Famines; that ſometimes the people did not know where (for drought) to find water, nor where (for neceſſity and hunger) to find bread.

4. Do we think Invaſion of Forreigners

(g) In 1530 *after a Comet is an Innudation of Tyber over* Rome; *and* Holland *and* Zealand, *had the like by the Sea, overflowing* 404 *Pariſhes.*

(*) *Anno* 1567. *A Comet at Sun-ſet in* Germany, 6 *Countreys over-run with Famine.*

(which

which is another inſtance) to be a ſore and dreadful evil? Believe it, ſo it is. And if God ſhould make this wanton Iſland, that love *French* cuts and faſhions, to feel the effects of ſuch a Judgement, (*h*) Oh who can tell, but then we ſhall conclude, this was the language of that Star; ſuch prognoſticks preceded the like events in *Hungary*, and why not in *Brittany*?

4. (*) To be more particular; for it is impoſſible that my memory ſhould retain above an hundred inſtances; and I think, one Author doth produce (near) two hundred of this kind of reading. And therefore I can but ſmatter at it; and there are ſome examples fitter to be writ) In that year 1066 (*i*) the *Normans* invaded *England*: *Toſto* alſo (proſcribed before) peſtred and infeſted the Coaſts, both of *Kent* and *Lincolnſhire*, fell upon many places, deſtroyed many perſons, kept in a full body. King *Haro'd* did fight them (the laſt that was of the preceding *Danes*,) he is conquered that

---

(*h*) *And ſmart by French cut-throats, ſo like to invade us at leaſt in Ireland.* (*) H. Alſtede *in Cometography* (*i*) Joh. Speed *Chronicle pag.* 404 *on April* 24. *A Comet ſeldom a ſign to Kings of fortunate ſucceſs.*

was the poſſeſſour: (for conqueſt was often the ſtrongeſt plea) the invader proves Conqueror, but great was the diſtreſs that hereupon followed This now is apparent in thoſe Chronicles and Hiſtories (if any have a mind to read) of thoſe times: and in other Hiſtories, there are ſuch plentiful inſtances of this kind, relating to ſuch dreadful Judgments, by invaſions and Comets preceeding, that it were needleſs to inſtance farther. But what you may have even from *Rome* to give in witneſs plenarily to this: in the year 410 (k) (after Chriſt) was a ſword-like Comet. O the ſad events it portended. The *Goths* and *Vandals* fell upon *Rome*; ſacked the City, laid that waſte, deſtroyed moſt of the places and Villages round about; (no age ever knew the like to't,) kept it and poſſeſt it for a conſiderable time. And ſo the wantonneſs of Chriſtianity, and the heighth and Pride of the *Roman* Papacy, that was then creeping, and almoſt crept up; was under the Plague and Puniſhment of Gods vengeance, and the *Goths* and *Vandals* Sword.

I note it for this; to let you ſee, that if

(k) *Anno*, 410. *Fulfit Cometa enſiformis & tanta erat hominum cædes, hoc tempore: quantam ætas nulla, a condito mundo novit.* All *Aſia*, *Africa*, and *Europe*, to Eaſt and Weſt felt it.

God have a mind to plague and punish a people, he can fetch a Nation, (1) North or South, East or West, from any side, flank or border of us, (Gods Troopers can muster any where,) and make great and destructive work of us: at least to prove a long scourge.

5. Shall we say that Pestilence is a dreadful Judgment, God knows, (Remember -65) so 'twas; so it is alwayes where it comes. (It brings terrour round about) There are instances in my poor reading of Ten or a Dozen Comets that have appeared in the world (before it, in various Lands and Cities.) And then in a year or two, as the Patience of God and the Prayers of the Godly did obtain.) God sent the Famine and dreadfullest Pestilence, that (*triennum duravit,*) was rampant three years together in *Europe,* to the depopulation of many Cities and Towns. So that it were to little purpose to instance particulars: This is reported by *Historians* so

---

(1) Caldea *was above 4 Months march from* Judea, *but yet invaded it with Gods Troops: as* Hab. 3. 16. * Lam. 2: ult (m) *t medio sepetientium, vivi adhuc spiritum trahentes, cum mortuis sepelirentur; t' e expiring were buried with the dead,* Anno 1006.3 Anno Hen. II. *Imperatoris.* A. Alsted.

large

largely; that in one place my Author faith, that the Living were weary of burying the Dead; the Dead were so naucious and burthensome to them, that both were interr'd together.

6. Shall we say in the last place, (for I'le go no further in this first branch) That the death of Princes is a great plague? Sometimes truly, so 'tis, especially if those have been in any kind real favourers of Religion and the Christian Doctrine, or the Kingdom of Christ. Stories tell us, about 337, 'twas in *Constantines* latter end, a great Comet appeared a little before his death; and shortly after, he expired, and yeilded the conquest of the Grave, (*n*) for that's a Master that will fetch down a Princes Scepter, (tho' never so good) as soon as any thing in the World: Well, but how immine and innumerable evils did bode to Christians and Christianity, after this great mans death, is easie to read. So great a Favourer, that Emperour was, and Protector of Religion? The dangers and Perils that attended Christians also at *Theodosius*'s death, (*o*) are not easily to be exprest:

(*n*) *Three of his Sons strove for Succession and Christiani Immanibus periculis expositi.* (*o*) *Anno Dom. 454. Theodosius dyed but of Julians and Nero's end, and others, I need say less, their Comets foretelling the worlds better hap in an exit of their Tyranny.*

All presag'd by Comets; the latter Comet lasted 10 weeks.

In this last effort of Judgment, (predicted or witnessed by preecedaneous Comets;) I read my self almost weary; and begun then to think of numbring, and in one Author told to the number 7, and saw, that grew upon me, so I thought it in vain to go on.

In another Author I went to number and there it came to the number of Eighty Princes, or Eighty odd, that at home, and abroad went off with Comets.

If then you dare give me credit, 'twere easie to produce vast Examples of the mighty hand of God, (who is higher * then the highest) upon some great ones, especially viceous Princes. As touching *Vespatian*, (and he was none of the worst;) as touching *Nero*, both his beginning and his Exit was reported to the World, by Comets in the Heavens, so both the pious and flagitious have omens; As if God would say, now you shall have a great Persecutor to rise; (setting aside only the five first (p) years of *Nero*, in which he put on humanity; but paid it off with Barbarism and (q) Bruitism (his Reign *merum latroci-*

---

* Eccl. 5. 8. (p) Neronis *quinquenium* (q) Styld the first Dedicator of Christian blood, by Martyrdom.

nium)

cinium (bruitism at last.) And a little before his death, then God also presignifies his destruction (as I said) by another witness in the Heavens. So that Tyrant dyed, *more majorum*.

This may be said of *Comodus*, another Emperour. The like of other instances. Here we might come into *France*; there into *Spain*; Here into our own Countrey.

There are sometimes five or six particular instances of Princes and Princesses fall after a Comet; and some of them particularly foretold by divers other Portents. As for instance, Queen *Marys*, the great † Abettor and Promotor of *Popery* here in *England*; and her death and 24 more was foretold a little before by a Comet. I name this for one thing : You should not think much for once, if I mention a passage out of a strange Author ; (but yet, it may be, you have heard of it :) there was one *John Gadbury* in 65, that wrote a Book concerning Comets; whether the same that is so notorious now in the Plot, I cannot say, but this is the passage for which I cite it : (you'l excuse it when you Read it ;) God (saith he) and nature intended, that

---

† *A Comet* Anno 1558. *in the form of a Spit* (*the most.*) *in August*) *of a pale envious colour, nine Princes, Fifteen Cardinals all dye, soon after.*

the Death of the Princes should not have the Knells of Church Bells on Earth, they be not sacred enough for such illustrious performances, but it shall be signified by a Knell from Heaven, (or Comets, as in the 44 page, of that book:) Whether from reverence to his Prince, or to his *Roman* Faith, or of Love to Mrs. *S.* or to his Doctrine of calculation of Nativities, Sir *R. P.* may tell better then I.

To all might be added great mutations in States, Massacres, Seditions, decollations, &c. great changes in Religion, for the worse, sometimes for the better. But one Author comfortably ends it with this word, with which I'le end this first branch.

Notwithstanding all this, (saith he) *there are* (r) *better things to be hoped to come afterwards.*

Now, as for the second Branch, that these are signs, (more frequently of Evil I grant, witnesse those Judgments forementioned ; so) Secondly, But they are also Tokens and Signatures of Good.

It is not so much to be collected from the form, nature, course (or current) of the Comets which God makes new in the

---

(r) *Quibus meliora succedere speranda.*

Heavens; for sometimes those have divers Forms, and Shapes, and Colours; yet do never jump in one and the same Issue and effort, in any of the said Judgments I have mentioned. But this is a Subject of a consolatory nature; and I am loath to speak more now upon this Subject; but willing to postpone my second design, and the instances of good coming, to the Use of Consolation (in the Conclusion of the fourth part.)

The second thing I was to signifie, was by Induction, to prove that as several Judgments of God are consequents unto such signs; so there are several years in ages past, which have produced both the sign, and the thing signified.

But this now would put me upon a more particular elabourate History from some years before Christ, and since to the present time: (further my Authors lead me not) There is one, (I hear) hath writ the History of all the Comets, since the Creation. But in one Dr. *H. Alstede*, I find some * years before Christ, six Comets recorded, and the rest after Christ do make

---

* *A. M* 3519. *The* Peloponesick *Wars ensued, A. M.* 3798. *post mortem Demetrii. A. M.* 3947. *de quo* Sybil. Aug. *hic puer major te est.*

up till now neer two hundred Comets. (*) (of one, that *Sybil* to *Auguſtus*.)

You would not therefore expect that I ſhould run over all theſe particular inſtances again; for what I have given of the ſevere Judgments, which God hath inflicted upon the ſinful world and the holy City, (*Euſeb. p.* 53.) after ſuch ſigns; ſuffices only to prove what I deſign; *(viz.)* the dreadful omens to the wicked; and comforts to the pious, that do iſſue upon ſuch wonderful and prodigious ſigns. Only in ſhort view.

1. *Anno* 69. A Comet as a flaming Sword is ſeen over *Jeruſalem*, portends its ruine.

2. *Anno Chriſti* 78. At *Cyprus* ſeen a Comet: Many Cities overturned by Earthquakes.

3. Comet 195. *Severus* dyed.

4. *Anno* 323. That Hereſie of *Arrius* ſprings up.

5. *Anno* 1529. A ſweating ſickneſs on the *Engliſh*. 4 Comets in that year.

5. *Anno Chriſti*, 1539. The heat dryes up Fountains, and burns the woods.

6. Two Maſſacres in *France*, follow the ſecond Comet, one *Anno Dom.* 1572.

(*) *Illa perdixit Chriſtianam Religionem ſignificare.* 7. *Anno*

7. *Anno* 1652. *John Cotton* of *N.E.* dyes, our changes by *O.C.* Protector, the long Parliament dissolved, *Scot. and* invaded and subdued.

Therefore, since the former of these branches supplys the latter; I will now pass from the Doctrinal part, and proceed to something more practical; and so, I think, (to a vulgar auditory) I may be more acceptable. And there are three uses.

If God gives signs of sometimes sad, sometimes glad events to come in the world; Then it may be,

First, For Terrour.
Secondly, For advice.
Lastly, For comfort.

First, I say for Terrour. It is a passage I find in one Author, cited out of *Voetius*, (the Book I have not) * concerning prodigies or wonders *paveant Impii.* Let the wicked fear and tremble; If sinners will not fear, God hath an art (and a powerful one) to make them both fear and feel.

Keep this Rod (saith God unto *Moses*) for a Token against the Rebells, mark that passage, *Numb.* 17. 10. For *Aarons*

---
* Voetius *de O[s]tentis.*

Rod Bloſſomed and Budded, well (faith God) I am reſolved to convince theſe Rebells, one way or other; and that they may know there is a diſtinction betwixt them, and my Servant *Aaron*; keep this Rod (faith he, to *Moſes*) in the Tabernacle of Witneſs in the Ark : *Heb.* 9. 4. as a Token againſt the Rebells. * God ſends Tokens then ſometimes againſt rebellious and wicked ones, ſuch was that *Dan.* 5. to *Beltſhazar* in's carouſing, when the Lord would reprove *Eli* for the wickedneſs of his Two Sons ; this ſhall be a Sign (faith he.) Mark ; (He doth it by a Sign.) A word of * an Angel, a Prophet, a *Samuel* would not do't ; well, I'll pay him off (though I break Heart and Neck at once) (faith God) and his whole houſe to boot. And therefore this ſhall be a Sign (faith God by Young *Samuel*) thy Two Sons † *Hophni* and *Phinehas* ſhall die both of them in one day. God hath wayes to ſhew Signs of diſpleaſure; and it is a mercy he'll tell us by a word; but if we will not hear, being (as *Eli*) his own: Then we muſt feel, For God will not looſe his own.

---

* *Wonders are oft for unbelievers,* 1 Cor. 14. 23. * 1 *Sam,* 2. 27, c. 3. 18. 20. † 1 *Sam.* 2. 34.

I tell

I tell you, Sirs, it is the moſt dreadful thing in the world, (if God is ſo ſevere with Saints) to be an Impenitent Atheiſt, when God is preaching by ſuch Signs, for as there is ſomething of wrath, (s) (O yee *Herodians*) againſt that which muſt fall; ſo their is ſomething of Grace and Favour hinted to us, in that which ſhall riſe and never fall, That's the Kingdom of Chriſt, yea and Chriſt will carry it at laſt. Therefore ſinners ought to fear and tremble at the Signs that God ſets above, you cannot (by a huff and a ſcoff) hector down one of theſe Signs, out of the Orb, where God hath ſet it.

Thoſe that write the Hiſtory of Comets, tells us, that in moſt of the Spheres: (or in the beſt Philoſophy-language of the Scripture call'd the Stories in the Heavens, *Amos* 9. 6. which ſome expound, of the Spheres; *Hebr. Aſcents.* though others diſpute it) they ſay, in moſt of theſe Stories, Comets have been ſeen, excepting the ninth Sphere of Heavens, and that of 1572 pertain'd to the Eighth Orb where

---

(s) *Si præſepe vagientis Herodem ita terruit, quid tribunall judicantis.* If one in the Manger did ſo terrify, what will the Tribunall of Chriſt do?

onely

onely the fixed Stars are; they say these the number of Two Twousand and 23 and some 300 have been since discovered by Navigation. And yet that Star which we read of in 1572, (so much disputed about, if a Comet or no?) was seen (*in Sydere Cassiopei*) not a wandring Star, but a fixed Star: as 3 more by some are also called new Stars (*viz.*) In 1604, 1607, and 1618. but dreadful were the effects, and Issues that followed upon them all: and perhaps the world is not yet deliver'd of their Events.

If the world will not know; nor believe, nor fear; I, (saith God,) I have a way to open their deaf ears: let them be as *Surdi*, and absurd as they please, they may keep this Deafness, till the last Trumpet sound, if they can: but they'l before that often tingle. For, certainly God will make the Hearts of the most Atheistical Ones, to gripe and quake : 'Ere all the Scene is finisht.

What shall God preach by his Word, and by his Works; and all for his Son, his Kingdom, his Name, Gospel, and People? And shall both word and works be hectored out of the World (and the Heaven's too) by a company of swash Bucklers, and Atheistical Villains, that scarce know or own any thing of the Language

guage and Works either of God or his Signs, aright? O! why should the world be so mad, as to play with edged Tools? can sinners find nothing to jest with, and be joakers † or scoffers about, but the Language of such Glorious, and new Created Witnesses or Ministers that God sets up beyond the reach of any Humane Arm? No, no, certainly, this Spirit, if it be not cured; (and that's very hard) 'twill be plagued and cursed, wheresoever God finds it: so was *Herod* that set Christ at nought * and mocked him. I'll tell you a passage or two of a Huffer; of such *Peter* prophesies there shall be in the last times, Mockers, Scoffers saying, where is the Promise of his coming? you tell us of Signs, and portents: why there was one Comet *Anno* 79 In *Vespasians* latter end, (for there was Signs then;) and there were others that wrote their presages, * and where is that you talk of? all comes to nothing, vanishes away. Hold; there appeared a Star

---

† ἐμπαῖκται Illusores, in 2 Pet. 3. 3. and *Jude* 18. ἐμυκτηρίζεται Gal. 6. 7. Luk. 23. 11. * Ille per jocum dixit pertinere hoc prodigium parthorum regi, qui comam nutriret. * Soon after he dyed.

in *Vespasians* time; one of his Wizards, or Courtiers told him, that it imported a change in the Empire, or the death of the Emperour; No, no, (saith he) I don't fear that: (perhaps it was *Stella Crinita*, a long haired Comet) it rather signifies the death of the King of the *Parthians*, because he wore long hair (*Vespatian* was bald,) but so it pleased God, *Vespatian* died *paulo post*, soon after, for all his scofing merry humour.

If men will scoff and jest with Heaven it self; he will not alwayes bear it.

Did I say, I would tell you of another? *Libanius* * a witty Sophister, asked a Poor Christian (In the latter part of *Eusebius*'s History in a jear against Christ.) what the Son of the Carpenter was now a doing: (this was about *Julian* the Apostates death: he was a dreadful Apostate from Religion, and the vilest scoffer the Earth bore) where now (saith he) is the Son of the Carpenter? (he meant Jesus) what does he do? In answer to this, this holy man said, he is making a * Coffin, to bury such scornful ones, as thou art; and presently afer he died; that (as *Saba*

---

* *Eusebii Trip. hist.* 441. and of *Theodor.* p. 769.
* *Sandapilam concinnatur ille faber Eusеb. ut super.*

said)

said) had so wasted Christs Vineyard.

Oh! who knows, but God is telling us of a Coffin, by the dark vision of this strange, and wonderful Star now expired? For when they are out, (saith an Author) their effects are not out, † but that I think, my auditory hath not so vain an Atheist as this was, that needs, or suits such a discourse as this; I could be content to fill up my time in this just reprimand. For the World is grown to that height of Atheism in all places; it appears in all hearts, it is frequent in all Mouths.

I will only pass off, this branch of the first use, with some (not Astrological Calculations; * but rather Theological, or Practicall) Observations of the Nature, and Course of that Star, so lately appearing to every eye.

Did you observe the motion of it, from the † East to the West, (inclining Northward?) that is the motion of the Sun. Then I apply it only thus, (by way of Similitude) Does that false and abominable long tail'd Religion (I mean the Romish) Run all the day the same course that the Son

---

† *In Gods time, though as Cardan said Corpora Cœlestia non agunt in instanti.* * *Some notes conjecturall of this Comet in particular.* † *In its course all the day.*

of God did *(*Jesus Christ himself, our Sun of Righteousness*)* pretending to derive from; yet persecuting of him in his Gospel and interest from East to West: and so to overspread all *Britain* by a bloody conspiracy, that finds some room northward, never such a tail'd comet; so never so envious a Horrid Plot and so fatal even to our English Parliaments; so threatning to command the whole World?

That Religion, before many years (I am sure, before many ages) will take (as this Star hath done) it's final Exit, and extinction, in darkness. It is a passage out of *Lactantius* * There is a word I must say (Thirteen Hundred years agoe, he prophesied it,) I fear to say it, (saith he) yet *I* must say it, what's that?

Romanum nomen, tolletur de terrâ.

The Name of *Rome* shall be taken out of the Earth. shall that faction aspire now under the course and government of a Protestant, and cross the lines and orders, that the Son of God (Christ's true Religion) hath in the Gospel drawn, that certainly will be extinct shortly, soe, it intimates

---
* Lact. *Li.* 7.

good

good, then (if I well measure its lines.) But I gather it more from the observation of Scripture and Divinity, (the best discovery of the works of God.)

If you'l observe next, this Star had a long Tail, the longest (I grant,) save one, I hear or read off.) And I read of four or five of that kind, in other Authors we (should love to study the works of God;) and it is but for this once (on such a Subject) that I think to treat.

Those that have such long Tails; they seem to presignifie long, sad, and doleful effects. Why the Lord himself in the form of it doth witness, that he threatens the whole world, with a Brush, or a Rod, as long as 36 degrees in the Heavens. But I am not exact in that observation, (as to the degrees.) But this I mean (by way of resemblance tropologically,) that God hath certainly for some a long Rod, and its lifted up: Whereas most of the Comets that have yet been in the World, have rather had their Tayles asloap; or like a Goat, (*Stella barbata*) with the beard downward; and they say, they that have the brush erect upwards, are most dreadful and ominous; then it signifies that God hath a wonderful Brush, and long Rod set up in the Heavens, to lash some that com-

mon

common hands reach not, for certainly they that are so long, may reach every back, and every where, and who are they that so long an Arm and Rod will not reach? Shall I say,

Thirdly, (For I think God should make nothing in the Heavens, but we should aim and conjecture at the signature of it; (as the *Magi* did at Christs star here,) though the time will best prove the Issue.

Did you observe that the colour was exceeding envious? (if I may so call it.) for they say, that those that are of a *Saturnian* colour, they signifie like himself, envious effects. Why then it signifies, O the envy, blood and mischief of the Confederators, and machinations, if not Massacres and Assassinations that may attend our times before the root, and top of this Plot be fully lop't and punished.

How hard a thing is it to root out Plot and Plotters! Still the dark envious eye of the *Roman* Religion is upon the poor Protestant. Therefore it should set us a watching, least they serve us as *Coligni*, Sir *Edm. Godfrey*, Justice *Arnold*, Mr. *Pye*, and others; and who knows what blood may follow, *Jam.* the 2d.

Quis-

*Quisquis ab exilio regnabit sanguine mul-
to.* Speed.

He that from Exile comes again,
He'le surely have a bloody Raign.

And if I may be bold so far, (though I think that they observe right, that *post pone* the effects and events, one or two years, or more; Yet) I find at the same time, or a little while after, some Issues, or consequences, have spoken the Language in part of these appearances. What hath been produced now upon this Star: (to impose I will not be so bold and peremptory; yet) give me leave, (since I am upon't) to go on a little.

If *I* have not been much abused, (and *I* would not easily take things upon common report) that there was one in the West-Countrey spake slightingly of this Comet, as if there was nothing in it; They asked him wherefore he said so? sayes he, *If I* * do not believe as *I* say, let my eyes fall out; and it is said, one, if not both of his

---

* I *heard of the Letter and all particulars, (and could not obtain it, as yet:) by a sober person.*

eyes

eyes fell out before the next morning with great pain ; some both sober and pious, saw the names of both the person and place. (And if common fame doth abuse us, it may abuse you as well as me.) But *I* make it my care to observe the works of *God* (and judgments) as well as *I* can, by the truest information. For these two Months or more that this Comet hath appeared in the Heavens; *I* cannot accurately say how long, because the first sight at its beginning, is so hard to find, in its dark language, is so dark: yea, o! how many of our Preachers have been silenced that little time? (*I* mean by death.) I have observed 3 or 4 of late ; thirteen, or fourteen, within a few months at least ; but that which makes me speak of it, is this ; that by a worthy and pious Minister, I was told (if Fame and the Letters, abuse us not from *Paris*.) That a Minister of *Charington* (†) nigh *Paris* in *France*, (where the persecution is so raging, meets the Host, (so some :) others say, by the rabble excited on a Religious account) but they came upon him, and knockt him oth' head, and trod him it was said to death ; but he after recover'd, But if we should come to our own course of Affairs here is a Parliament first Prorogued, and then Dissolved;

(†) Mr. *Chude*.

and

and what that Diffolution will be attended with ; God knows. Truly, fometimes I fear, that one Diffolution after another ; one fick Convulfion after another, muft needs fpeak fad. For, as it is with the Body Natural, when it is Sick ; it lyes one while, this way : then turns to that fide, and then a tother fide ; fo we lye of this fide, and turn a tother fide but ftill the difeafe is within. And now the cry is 41, and for *Oxford*; and (fay fome) you'l bring it to * 41. the Nobles obferve that place has oft been Fatall, who brings it to 41 ? (I wifh Popifh Councels be — not — at the Helm,) But I bring it for this that you may fee how neer things jump and Councels concurr, with fuch portents God has fet in the Heavens.

These things are fomething clofe and practical : and *I* hope pertinent ; and God muft make them Profitable and Powerful. There are two things yet behind.

Firft in Dehortation.
Secondly, Exhortation.

Firft, Doeth God fet old and new ftars,

---

* *From 40 to 31, is inclufive near to 41.*

(or Comets) in the Heavens, to lisp out, or hint his own mind? O then! take heed of slighting even the least Messenger from God, that brings us to our knees! *(t)* or to enquire at his oracle, Lord, what shall be the end of these things? (as *(v) Daniel* saith, Lord (saith *Baalam*, tho' a Conjurer) who shall live, when God doeth this? Mark how awakened and sensible these men were (the good and bad, and *Daniel*, especially) and say Lord what is it? or when shall be the end of these wonders? Take heed of that the *Philistims* Priests feared, 1 *Sam.* 6. 2, 6, 9. slighting any signature of Gods wrath. It's said *Job.* 36. 31, 33. of the Heavens, (the Lords Tabernacle) its noise shews of it, and verse 31. by them he judgeth, that is, (by loud signs,) what sin deserves, see also *ch.* 37. *v.* 4, 5, and and 12, 13. If you have a letter from a Friend, and you know the Seal, why you cannot but expect, here's some signification, word or Token from my Friend, and therefore you are very careful of the Letter, Sign and Seal, so God teaches *Job* natural Philosophy, *v.* 4, 5, and 12, 13. out of the *Ætherial* Bodies and the influences of them, (see also *ver.* 14.—16. and

---

(t) 1 Pet. 1. 11. (u) Dan. 12. 6. 8. Numb 24. 22.

ch.

ch. 38. *v.* 7, 14. It's turned as Clay to the Seal. (*i. e.*) by their motions, the morning fets a Seal and turn on the Earth.

Here's a Seal (faith God) in the Heavens, but it is a dark one ? but what will you fay ? why you fhould greatly reverence that hand, by which it is fealed. Speak not flightly of God and his wonderful works; Gods Tokens were dreadful to the Heathens, *Pf.*65.8. For then you fpeak flightly of his word; and there his works are beft decypher'd. Fear and tremble rather * if thefe things won't do, he hath Snow and ten times more treafures of Hail referv'd for the wicked, as *Job.* 38. 23, 24. that fhall make the Atheiftical Worlds ears tingle. I'le work a work fhall make his ears tingle that hears it. As 1 *Sam.* 3. 11. of *Elies* doom, fo 2 *King.* 21. 12. on *Manaffeh*'s, *Jer.* 19. 3. on *Jerufalem.*

2. The fecond is, As we fhould not flight and contemn them; fo, we fhould not fear them. Friend, Art thou afraid of the figns of * Heavens ? That's like a Heathen. No, fear thy * God, and avoid what provokes his difpleafure. A good man ftept out when there was a wonderful Thunder

---

* *As Caligula, that at Thund.r crept into holes*
† *See Jer.* 10. 2.

and Lightning; faith he, this is my God, Paternal Interest takes of Terrour.

There are dreadful things foretold; what? can you say? by sure interest; and by found Faith, truly, this is my God? And what! afraid of the Stars? *Jer* 10. 2. doth expresly forbid it. Be not dismayed at the signs of Heaven, for the Heathen are dismayed at them. What though these are doleful signatures? What though there are dreadful things coming (at hand) upon the Earth? Yet fear God. As he said † if thou wilt offer an offering, offer it to the Lord; foe, if thou wilt fear, fear and worship God: as *v*. 8. the *Magi* did Christ.

The Third and last is, Take heed of over-reverencing, Take heed of worshipping any of these Creatures, or effects of Gods power. They shew their Makers Wisdom, but shew nothing of Worship due in that case; That is dangerous; see *Deut*. 4. 19. And lest thou lift up thine eyes to Heaven, and when thou seest the Sun and the Moon, and the Stars, even all the Host of Heaven, shouldest be driven to worship them, 2 *Chron*. 33. 2, 5. &c. so the Heathen worshipped all the host of Heaven: which yet do all worship God,

---

* Judg. 12. 15. † Jer. 8. 2, *and* 19. 13. *Also Psal.* 147. 3. *called to praise him.*

as *Neh.* 9. 6. Now, whether they be old Stars or new; whether they be Angels; or whatsoever Creatures they are, they are Creatures not fit to be worshipped; that's Popery: Do as the wise men here did; they had a mind to worship him; (*Herod* pretended so; but never intended it; his design was to worry to destroy him:) But these poor wise men, they ascribe divine Worship to a poor Babe, *v.* 8. They don't worship the Star. It is true, they were glad when they saw it; but they came, and opened their Treasure, and worshipped him; for when (tho' the Star brought them thither, they did not worship the Star all the way;) they worshipped Christ the Babe of Glory, and saw him to be a deserving one to be worshipped. (y) Worship not any thing that your eyes see. Take heed then of the Doctrine of a breaden God, which is of the Priests-making. Away with that odious Idle of the heast, or breaden God, made by a few Lattin words of a Priests, that's Popery: and withal, our bowing, kneeling, cringing at a Rail-table Symbolical Popery. Though the Bread be a

---

(y) *Aurum, Thus, Myrham; Regique, hominiq; deoq;*

Sacramental sign of Chrifts real prefence: yet to be bow'd too, no more then the Star that lead to Chrift.

Oh then, how like to interpretative Idolatry, (or as theirs (of and) at the Calf:) is ours, that kneel to the fign, yet deny the real prefence (by't) fignify'd, how fay Papift of us?

(*adore*, Which whilft the Bread and Tables they Deny the real prefence; there, before.

The like caution lyes in the cafe of rites, geftures, and *Romifh* geniculations, Altars, Veftures, and places that derive from Popery: and all to be null'd, (as chips of that old block:) As to places I end with that of old *Hyiarion, Male ecclefiam dei in adeficiis, tectisq; veneramini.*

So Ends the Third Part.

The

The Fourth and laſt part.

Matth. 2. 2, 9, 10.

IT was a new work, and a new Covenant, and a new King, that *G*od was now exhibiting in the World ; the Signature whereof, he was pleaſed *(*as divers Authors I could cite, do call it*)* to make out by a new Star, *(*)* He that had in the firſt work of Creation, made ſo many Stars ; (and did fix them in their ſeveral Orbes) is pleaſed now, to make one *S*ingular and *S*pecial Star, placed in a lower Region; but for a higher and more noble end *(vid :)* to conduct theſe Wiſe Men (the firſt fruits of the *Gentiles)* unto the Knowledge and Sight of Chriſt. From whence we have concluded.

(*) Dr. Mayer, *and* VVard *in locum.*

When God is about some Great Work, or to Exhibit a new King and Kingdom in the World; he makes some strange new and Glorious Appearance of it; (as a Sign) in the Heavens.

I grant he's not limited to Stars or Comets in Heaven for there be many sorts of Prodigies and they seldom or never come alone.

In prosecution of which, *I* have gone thus far, to shew you in the former three Discourses, what Methods *G*od hath taken, to discover his Mind, by these new and prodigious appearances, in what lines or signatures, and by what instances, or examples the thing appears by the experience of all ages by past to be a truth.

Now there still remains something of the most practicall and useful part of the discourse; which was first in intention: though last in expression. To wit, in two special uses; Partly Admonition, Partly Consolation. There was one thing dispatched the last part; and that was for Terrour. What remains of that (that slipt our Memory then) will be subservient to what follows in this last part; and therefore *I* will not rehearse, nor recapitulate

tulate at all. fo then, my work is two fold at this time.

Firſt, to lay down what admonitions may be fignified by fuch Signs. And,

Secondly, what Confolation (if any) can come out of fuch terrible Signs, and truly, there fcarce ever was is, or will be that thing in the world, that had not fome comfort in the end.

It is partly Caution, or Dehortation; take heed of flighting thefe Prodigies: There are none of *Gods* words, (nor his works neither) that it becomes his Creatures to flight, and to fpeak of them as ridiculous, to vilepend the workmanfhip and Opperation of Gods hands. is to reflect on the Maker. *If* thou didſt but fee a Devil (with all the Chains of Darkneſs about him) appearing in fome dark and terrible place; would it not awe, and affright? And yet the Devils were Angels, and are *Gods* Creatures: (though now his Prifoners, for they have fallen from their firſt good ſtate) why then fhould any of the things (any part of the Workmanfhip of *God*) be flighted or infignificant (that have the like Terrour.) *I* added,

2. Take heed of fearing them. (in a flaviſh manner) That's the errour on the one

hand

hand; this, on the tother, *(b)* fear none of thofe things that you fee; for, behold their Language is (could they fay it out,) as the Angel faid to *Manoa*; if thou wilt offer an Offering; offer it to the Lord. or, as the Angel to *John*, Worfhip God, Fear God. *(c) Rev.* 19. 10, 22, 8. Never any fuch dreadful fights were; but (what ever good might follow afterwards, yet) evil did immediately bode firft, and good fucceeded. As therefore we ought not to flight: fo we ought not to be terrified with any fuch thing; though it be a Sermon, and a Preacher of Judgement. Gods Minifters are called Stars; they are bound to preach both Judgment, and after Mercie; Gods Signs in the Heavens do fo fometimes (moft ufually) They Preach Wrath, and Judgement; yet be not afraid: if thou wilt fear; fear the Maker of them.

There was a difpute (upon the appearance of a Star, or Comet) betwixt *Charles* the great *(d)* (fo called) the Emperour; and *Egenard* a *Philofopher*; * and becaufe

---

(b) Pfal. 119. 43. 52, 120, 157. *There's hope, and comfort, and help too for one that trembles, at both Rod and Word. (c) Jud.* 13. 16. *ut fupra (d) A. Dom.* 814. * *He fear'd, mutationem regni mortemque principis portenderet.*

he

he found the *Emperour* suspicious, that that Comet appearing a little before, foretold a change in his Death, the *Philosopher* put on the place † of a Divine, (saith my Author) and laboured to comfort the *Emperour*, and did exhort him by this Text that I named before in *Jer.* 10. 2. *Be not afraid of the Signs of Heaven, of which the Heathen are afraid.* But the *Emperour* (piously affected) gives him this answer ; though we ought not to fear these Creatures ; (e) yet we ought to fear the Creator of them and us ; for he is pleased (when he will express his Anger and Displeasure for Sin) to reprove our sloath, by such dreadful Signs in the Heavens, so saith this Pious *Emperour.* And therefore we ought to take it as a great Mercie : we ought not to fear them. neither (lastly) should we worship them.

This was the Errour of the Heathen ; it flowed from the Devil, to worship the Creature , that appears in Gods service, and stead ; this was ever *Satan*'s design,

---

† *Locum Prophetæ adducens ait A signis Cœli nolite timere.* (e) *Non aliud timere debemus nisi illum qui nostri et illius sideris, est Creator. qui nostrum inertiam talibus indiciis admonere dignatur nam omnes comuniter tangunt.* &c. *Alsted. Pag.* 488.

that he might place himself behind the Curtain, and so steal away that worship that's onely due to God, who intrudes in Gods place, that he may pass for God: in the Oracle: and so becomes the God of this World. *Dr. Burthog Pag.* 346.

If you say, that Christians (Gods People) are in no danger of this; then, I answer, why did Satan tempt Christ to Worship him? *Math.* 4. 8, 9. If no danger to us? and what meant *Moses*? *Deut.* 4. 18. saith he, lest thou lift up thine eyes unto Heaven, and when thou seest the Sun, and the Moon, and the Stars, even all the Host of Heaven thou shouldst be driven to worship them, and serve them, which the Lord thy God hath divided unto all Nations under the whole Heaven. The Sun Moon, and Stars are divided for the service and use of all Nations of the Earth, and therefore nor thou, nor any of them, are bound to worship them, for to worship them is to serve our servants.

I the rather propose these **Negatives**; because they are inlets unto the affirmative part of the Admonition. And this is two fold.

Be (positively) perswaded, First, to consider, Secondly, to prepare.

2. *Use of Exhortation*, 1. *consider humbly.*

First, I say, to consider the Signs of the Heavens, those that are fixed; or those that are (*de novo*) brought to sight. There is one Author that gathers up all the Comets, or semblear Stars from Christ, another from the Creation (for they are like Stars; carry the same Light, the same Use: the same, or greater Magnitude, then many of them; onely they are not the same in duration:) now I say, there is nothing that you can see: in Heaven, or Earth, but you ought to consider it. It is a dreadful thing to neglect this duty. Because they consider not the Opperation of his hands; therefore he will destroy them, and not build them up. Such a threatning in the *Psa.* 28. 5. And another like to it in the *Isa.* 5. 12. See two Witnesses, and both respect the Operation of Gods hands. God would do so and so to the Princes, * the antient, the honoura-

---

* *Hen. Alsted Exelius.* * *Tho. Trigg Pag.* 27. cites one Luc. Gauricus *this, multi ex inopinato* (*Anno* 1672. 77.) *a magistratu deponentur, et tantis calamitatibus conquassati, ut quo vertant ignorent: provideant ne ab hostium insidiis indigantur.*

ble;

ble; and why? Because they considered not the operation of his hands. Sometimes (saith God) I'le go to work by a Prophet, where that will do, I'll save blowes. When it wont't; then saith God, I le go to work.

And sometimes he works or makes appearances in heaven, sometimes in the earth, sometimes in the Clouds, sometimes in the Waters: Sometimes in one Element, sometimes another; all's the operation of Gods hands. There are (I am told) of Opinion, that Comets (it is not affirmed possitively) may be the operation of the Devils hands. I would be loth to make the Devil a Creator, especially, to have such a Regency and Power of Operation in the Bodies of the Heavens, Gods creation and Chambers. He is the Prince (indeed — of the Power (*g*) of the Air, but it is above the Air that such Appearances are set (all, save this in *Mat.* 2.) and by that Argument, he would inferr, that this Star was the Operation of the Devil: So that Satan did conduct the wife men, and so the Devils Star, that was a Conducter to Christ; a bad Argument in Logick, and a worse in Divinity. But grant it, for the present,

---

(g) Eph. 2. 2.

there is no body that sees the Effects of Sathan's Power in the Air over storms, But if it ought to give caution and great admonition to us; how much more the Operation of the Lord? though he hath a great power, I dare not say, in these Comets: for I find no Scripture, nor no Author affirms it But in all these things, (where God shews the operation of his hands;) you and I are bound to consider it. I would never have undertook to insist so long upon this Text, (three or four discourses;) but for admonition of a sleepy Ossitant age, that makes shams and ridicules of any thing. Now here would be a large Field, not only to consider one Comet (that in our Text) or that of late,) (which are Semblar Stars,) in the expansion of the upper Regions. But to tye my self only to a few Meditations; (for you have work enough for Meditation and Consideration, in any fair, clear night.

Consider these Creatures, (and all the rest in their Orbs;) think with thy self, who made these things?

Consider them first in their maker. Did the Heavens create themselves? Did the Stars produce themselves? Do the Comets (that in every age appear) exhale themselves? For my own part, though I do

grant,

grant, that there is a power under God in nature, but God governs them all that first made them, that made nothing in vain; * (God, in, or by nature, I mean;) this we must conclude, that there is no appearance in the Heavens, but it (has a direct and long finger, to point us up to our Creator, * as that Star pointed the *Magi* (the wise men) to Christ; and never left them, till it brought them there. Which makes some say, 'twas an Angel of God; or some Divine Power from Heaven; others affirm it was the Spirit of God, (as I said before.) You may put them altogether if you will; for the thing could not of its own conduct do what it did, without some peculiar Voice dictating, or spirit from above.

2. *Diversity*, Consider not only the Maker as *Psal.* 33. 6. but the diversity of them by Gods word. See what a Glorious Heaven, (in a clear night) you may behold; how many eyes are there fixed upon you. Who can number that Host; (as God said to *Abraham*.) Look up,

---

* *Nunqam f.tilibus excanduit ignibus æther.* (i. e.) Manilius to Augustus.
We may not mock and gaze,
When Skyes with Comets blaze.
* *And this late Comet pointed us directly up.*

faith

faith he, and † consider if thou canst number the Stars of Heaven ⁓ (cited before) Then shall thy seed be numbred. As if God would exhibit the tydings of the new Covenant, (to his numerous seed,) by puting him on the Meditation of the Stars of Heaven.

3. *Their bigness.* Consider them in their magnitude, (besides their diversitie.) How many of them (if we would go to natural Philosophy) might be produced, by plain Mathematical Demonstration, *(g)* to be Scores, and Hundreds of times bigger, only the Moon excepted; that's 39 times less then this Globe of the Earth? And then think with your selves, Lord, what a mighty workman was he, that made such glorious and beautiful things to stand and shine in the upper Region, and in each of the Spheres? of which, they reckon nine, save only the ninth and last. To all may be added the Order and Har-

---

† *Mr. Fr.* Banfield *notes some that have numbred* 1000, *and* 70 *odd.* pag. 1.23 *and disapproves that art of vain Astrology.* pag. 116. *and so do I.*

(g) *As the Sun is* 166 *times bigger then this Earth; some nigh a hundred times The fixed Stars in the eighth Sphear, those of the first magnitude* 107 *times bigger, for they have* 6 *Magnitudes, that all to us seem but as Candles.*

I   mony

mony, (and also the Swiftness of them) to move so many hundred of Miles in one hour, that it's thought the Musick of them must needs be sweet. Our natural Philosiphy might be corrected and bettered, (I think,) as a pious man, Mr. *Francis Banfield* observes, I long to see a natural Scheme of a right Scriptural Philosophy. *He buildeth his stories in the Heavens,* (saith he) in *Amos* 9. 6. or his Spheres (as part the second.) And in another place he hath this passage; By his Spirit he garnisheth the Heavens, and all their Hosts (and by he formed the crooked Serpent. *Job* 26. 13. Hebr. שִׁפְרָה *Shiphrah ornavit* שָׁפַר *decoravit.*

Now when * any would embroider curious work; why, here they set a spangle, and there another. Here (saith God) I have enamel'd a glorious mansion: and above this rich Pavement shall be the seat of the blessed. Oh then what is man, to have that Canopy; his Foot-stool at last? And will not you consider such a glorious house, to which you are a going?

Now there is this reason, why such Stars as these, or transitory appearances

---

(†) *Viam illam lacteam bara illam creavi omnia signa cælestia.* * *Of Shaphar venustus, & gratus fuit.*

of Comets, should be considered; something more particularly beyond the rest: For those are fixed and abiding; These only shine for some little (*h*) time, and disappear, therefore ought to be considered (whilst in being, and not forgot.)

Those have their natural course; These have some supernatural use, and import (intent, or portent: call it what you will.) When God makes a work to last, that's still in view; but when he makes a peculiar work a transient Creature, (which is then to preach its last, and go off, as all Comets do,) why, it's greatly by all Creatures to be considered. And that you may see what the advantage of such Consideration, (rightly took in) may be; You may (first of all) see what *David* reapt by it. Lord, (saith he,) what is man? When I consider the Heavens; What part of the Heavens? He does not propose the most glorious light; (the Sun) but he proposes the lesser to Meditation: When I consider the Moon, and the Starrs; Lord, what is man? saith he. Why then, by consideration of such Workmanship as God hath made for nocturnal view, such low-

---

(*h*) *The largest is said to be near a year, (as that over* Jerusalem,) *the shortest but an hour 3 quarters.*

er Creatures are for some special use appointed; by consideration (I say) you may come to learn humility, self-abasement, and self-abnegation: It seems to be inferr'd thus; Lord, that thou shouldest make such a glorious and beautiful workmanship, in the upper World, for mans service, or contemplation and instruction! And therefore it teaches me humiliation, subjection to, and an holy admiring of God. When I consider, Lord, what is man? *Isaac* went out for that end, at Eventide, *Gen.* 24. 63.

2. But then there is this for advantage; (for it serves for warning, as well as humiliation.) When God creates new things, he may be said then to do, as a People that have an invasion, or insurrection? Why, you know they have certain Hills, on which Poles and Beacons are set: and by combustible matter, they fire the Beacons, to give warning to all places adjacent; of such nature and use, are our Comets. Why so, (saith God) will I do; I'le invade the world, with my Troop (k) to punish them for their sins: They have invaded my Heavens —— and I'le invade their peace. When God fires his

---

(k) *As Hab.* 3. 16.

Beacons,

Beacons, it greatly concerns his Creatures to ſtand and wonder, to conſider, to take warning, and caſt what to do, or to repent, that's the meaning.

All the warnings of God have ſome ſignatures of advice, that way. Saints, Repent of your Sloth, formality, ſleepineſs; there will come a diſpenſation that will awaken all the ſecure (*l*) Virgins with Terrour, when that voyce comes, it comes at Midnight ; Behold, the Bridegroom cometh, ah! if you and I, be found ſleeping; what a dreadful alarum will it be if our Cloaths be off, and ungirt or defiled, and we not trimmed up as the Bride, that made her ſelf ready. (*Rev.* 19. 6, 7.) we ſhall be unfit to meet him, or follow him ; (much more) to Feaſt at's Supper, and what a dreadful loſs will it be, not to be prepared, when the Bridegroom comes! Saints then are called to Repentance: as well as others : to rub their eyes and ſee, if they can find that Sign of his Second coming, it was ſtrange that the Star was ſpyed by none of all the *Jews*, ſave only the *Magi*, but I deem it was in wrath to them not to ſee, what poor aliens dayly ſaw, and follow'd.

(*l*) Math. 25. 5, 6.

I heard a man, when I was but a Scholar, (it was one Mr. *Simon* of *Manch.*) go up, and pray a great while, on a day of Humiliation (before the Wars in 41.) when he had prayed a great while, very seriously; he took only this advise for his Text, and short Sermon; O *England*! Repent; and repeated it again, and so return'd to Prayer, whatever the inclination, or impulse of that man was; I am not to say.

But this is our Sermon: these Signs and Beacons of Heaven; they speak, or at least by dumb, (yet broad) Signs, signifie and seal something to us what can it be (if it be not a warning?) O *England* repent! Mr. *Stewart* of *Dunaghor* in *Ireland* at's death, said thus: The broken Covenant of *Scotland* shall be renew'd, the formality of *Ireland* clensed, and the prodigality of *England* removed, and the Sons of *Saul* hung up before the Sun, what he said (about 38.) perhaps God may verifie afore 88. O *Germany*! repent; and *France* repent! all yee Princes (abroad or at home:) or hear your Knells.

And they say, this Star at *Rome*, was more prodigious to view there then in *England*, now it is gone; well, let all Persons, all Places, take themselves concerned ed to deprecate its tremendous confequents or look to bear them, take it as a warning from God, to exite and ſtirr you up to repent, Let the Princes Read *Jer.* 4. 3, 4, 8, 9. c. 6. 1, 2. Crying Crimes, will bring Perilous times.

When the Lord lifts np his Standard, as *Iſa.* 18. 3. ſhall we not ſee it? At what time I ſpeak to a Nation (ſaith he *Jer.* 18. 7, 9.) or to a People, to pluck up (*i. e.*) by War and Judgment; if theſe People repent; I'll repent of the evil. Oh what a tender God a penitent People would make? They are Signs: but they are not certain; there's only one reſerve in Gods heart: as once for *Nineveh*, Grace, * Godly wiſdom, a true penitencie, it will command the Heavens; it will command the God of Heaven, (ſo to ſpeak as, †) let the Signs be never ſo bad, the Iſſue will be good. A penitent people may eſcape, when the prophane and ſcornfull, will be involved in Judgment. *Dan.* 5. *Belſhazzar* had warning fair, in his Fathers caſe; but a Sign might perhaps and would (though dumb) awaken to Conſideration: No: *A mene Tekel*, he had on's wall, yet in vain.

---

* *Sapiens dominabitur aſtris.* † *Iſa.* 45. 11.

There is no place, where their line and language is not heard. *Pſal.* 19. 3. *(*urg'd before*)* the line points at the center; take the right meaſure or compaſs of Gods lines. The word ſignifies the Speakers mind and will, and ſomething of his hand approaching. Liſten to the word, that you may eſcape the blow. * He that will not hear muſt feel; and he that will not mind a Sign, ſhall be made a Sign. Mind it, and you'l find it for a Truth, and call it a propheſie, if you will, and *I* ſay't again he that will not mind a *S*ign *(*to obey it*)* ſhall be made a *S*ign, to others, for's contempt.

And in the whole, let this be the Iſſue and good concluſion; (for one may preach Chriſt and Repentance out of any thing.) Happy, yea thrice bleſſed are they, that ſo ſhall eſcape. Get your ſelves well wrapt in the Arms of Chriſt; and then, neither the ſigns of the Heavens, nor the ſignifications following them, will at all hurt you. It is a paſſage you'l find in that grave and worthy Mr. *Caryl*'s book; writing, I think in his Twelfth Volume, concerning

---

* *Mind it ye curled Hairy Satyrs ſayes* John Bainbrigg *on that Comet in.* 1618. *Pag. the* 30, *cut off the vicious locks, and prefer the baldneſs of penitent innocency, before the locks of your Iniquity.*

theſe

these Creatures, (the Stars,) he mentions one that was told, that he was in his Nativity under very bad signatures, and constellations. O saith he, but I don't mind that now, Why? why (says he) I have had a second birth since.

If the stars speak sad concerning the first birth, if Grace bring thee to a second Birth, now the sign is alter'd, so Mr. *Jos. Caryl.* on *Job.* 31. 33. see the place, p. 256. saith one, *sapiens & sydera regit*, and saith another, (*Astra regunt homines, sed Deus astra regit.*) The Stars have some Dominion on Earth, but it is an inferiour Dominion; for they are governed in subordination to the Superior, (so *Caryl* observes, *) and mans good: And a wise man he governs the Stars (under God) not the Stars him.

So then, true Grace with Godly wisdom, will change, invert and altar all the signatures of Stars with their influences; *n* which is both a motive wherefore we should not fear them; and also, wherefore we should

---

* *In* c. 38. 33. *by a word signifying to execute the judged.* (n.) *So the same Author in Pag.* 220. *Third Vol. c.* 9. 9. *cites* Philo jude opicio mundi. *God (sayes he) made Earth fruitful on the Third Day, Gen.* 1.11,13. *ere he made the Stars to influence it, to show that it depends on the Makers Power not on the Stars.*

in

in time of danger come to God in Chrift, by faving repentance; (for that's the new birth; by applying our felves to him) we fo efcape all the dangers themfelves, or at leaft, the evil of them. And then the next or fecond part of the Ufe, (in fhort) follows, (*viz.*)

When you have confidered, and think, now my Maker fpeaks fomething to me in particular ; fomething to *England* in generall ; fomething to the World : (for the Beacon is feen farr and near.)

2. *Prepare to meet God.* Why then, prepare for by thefe (and many other Signs) there's fomething fignified; God never makes any old thing in vain; (to be fure,) he never fets new Comets, or warnings in vain or to gaze on: O Lord, (faith *Jeremie*) thou haft fet thy Signs in Heaven, and among thy people, and other people (that threatned the King himfelf) the 32 of *Jer.* 20. Signs were among thy People; what elfe? other people, fo that we and other people are concerned in them. (*It* was urg'd before,) This was towards the Captivity, in the feige of *Jerufalem.* (*o*)

(*o.*) *verfe* 1, 2, 3, 4. *but* 6 *Months ere all were conquered.*

Why then, ought we not duly to confider, and to prepare? Per adventure, there will be no efcaping for fome Perfons (q) (of grandeur as *Zedekiah* was) the dreadful fignatures and fignifications of thefe appearances of God, and of his juft wrath: Peradventure, (if thefe be) the efcape will be very difficult, and very narrow. Peradventure, Gods Judgments, that now found as *Sinai*'s Trumpet, louder, and louder, that have been, are, and are like to be for fome courfe of time upon the Earth; (r) till he hath removed the finners out on't. If fo, then ought we not to prepare? my Friends and Countrey-men, be ye in readinefs. One Perfon may die by the Fire, as *Zimri* burnt himfelf, 1 *King* 16. 18. another by the Sword; and the Prophet *Zedekiah* roafted, 1 *King* 22. 24. another by the Peftilence: (a) One by this Judgment, another by that; one by an Enemy Domeftick, another by a Forreigner falls: *Ezek.* 14, 21. by one dreadful hand or other, fometimes all four forely concurr. And why? faith God, becaufe I will do thus, prepare to meet thy God, O *Ifrael, Amos* 4. 12. Becaufe I

(q) *That profane perfideous fubftitute, by covenant.* Ezek. 17, 18. *and* 21. 26, 27. (*) Pf. 104 35. Job 38. 13, 23. (a) *Jer.* 29. 17. 22. will

will do thus, I have said it, you are resolved in your course of sin; I am resolved in this course. Therefore thus will I do unto thee; and because I will do thus unto thee, prepare to meet thy God, O sinner. But a word, (and briefly hinted) will be sufficient to the Godly-wife, and ten thousand signifie nothing to the Foolhardy. God has strong bonds for all mockers: as *Isaiah* 28. 21, 22. I say then, that good advise is all our concern. Ye Kings suffer fairly a diminution of your Glory; least the Lords long Brush sweep it into the dust.

'Ye Nobles reform your Lives, Oaths, and Families: Remember the pious end of that once witty Atheist, Earl of *Rochester*; do as he did; or you'l do worse: Ye judges and Lawyers reform your delatory vexatious and costly course in tearing of the Widows Wooll that flyes to the Law for Justice: or remember the 42 Judges. Ye Prelates put off the 2 Horns of your Myters, persecute no more, the poor Dissenters, or look to dy as *Arundel*. Ye Parliaments, take of the edge of all persecuting Laws, and let all turn as (*Nineveh*) from violence: that desire to escape.

It is the concern of the great, and of the little,

little, from the Shepherd, to the meaneſt Sheep in the Flock, to be in a prepared poſture. The Wolves are abroad; the ſigns give indication; the alarm grows louder; the ſound of Gods ſeventh and laſt Trumpet will be the loudeſt that ever was ſounded in the World; which I take does commence at the witneſſes reſurrection, and is to be the next diſpenſation; but neither of them we have yet, (I doubt, ſome writers muſt in that take new meaſures, *Rev.* 11. 15.)But I tell you, there's a Trumpet to blow, that will certainly ſhake the heart, and tingle (or ſtun) the ears, and tear open the eyes of the moſt obdnrate Villains, and Atheiſts in the world; and this ſerves for the ſecond Uſe.

1. The Third and laſt (of the whole) I will now diſpatch: Terrible things do Iſſue out comfort in Gods way of preaching. And O that I could immitate him! And there is comfort to theſe two ſorts out of this Doctrine; Nay, out of this Text and Context; And the one is to *Jews*, and the other is to *Gentiles*.

There's comfort for *Jews*. They are not indeed fit to have or hear it yet; but yet it is very fit we ſhould hear it (that are to pray for them) for God hath yet a people

ple among them who shall believe, and be saved; Out of all dispute *all Israel shall be saved, Rom.* 11.26. God hath said it, (we may believe it.) And mark what the text saith to this; *Where is he that is born?* what? King; of whom? *King of the Jews.* VVhen Christ came first into the world; his design was to fetch home the Jewes. Go to my house first, to my lost sheep *Israel* first, (*Matth.* 10.6. with 15. 26, and *Joh.* 1. 11.) saith the father; so Christ said. *He came to his own, and his own received him not.*

Well now, they have suffered a long rejection, (that now is posting to a period of *Daniels* numbers;) but yet they are not totally cast off; they are beloved for the fathers sake, *Rom.*) 11. 28. I remember *Abraham* my friend, saith God; And shall I forget the seed of *Abraham* my friend? kindness (as in *Jonathan's* son) reaches the seed too, 2 *Sam.*9.1,7.) I'll have them in, be they where they will, God will certainly have a voice (or hiss) to call them, *Zach.*10.8. that shall call them home, and call them together, as by a great trumpet, *Isa* 27. 13, and then, great shall that day be (See more of this in the second part)
Then

Then shall the children of Judah, and the children of Israel be gathered together, and appoint themselves one head, (Who is that? why Christ) *and they shall come up out of the land; for great shall be the day of Jezreel,* Hof. 1. 11. And Chap. 3. 5.

2. *To Gentiles.* As it's comfort to the Jewes, so 'tis also to the Gentiles. Here the text speaks of both. VVho told of the Star? VVere they not the wise men of *Persia,* or of *Arabia?* and where doe they come? (*) they come to *Jerusalem,* they come to ask the question, *where is he that is born ikng of the Jews?* I, but alas! by going to *Jerusalem,* they lost the sight of their guide. Now I'll insert (it is not much a digression) what that famous (†) Bishop *Hooper* the Martyr, in the History of his Life, and Letters, (in *Foxes* Book of Martyrs) hath to this purpose; (he speaks it by way of upbraiding of the *Roman* Bishops, that then were rampant, in the *Marian* dayes. These wise men (saith he, to this sense, or better lines,) all

---

(*) *God will find wayes preternatural, Prodigious and wonderful, to call home his own by, if ordinary ones fail.* (†) *Acts and Mon.* pag. 1517. Cited again by Mr. Trapp *in locum.*

the

the time that they minded the conduct of of the starr; they were led a straight way towards Christ, when they would go aside to the Scribes, Priests and wicked lyers, the Clergy of *Jerusalem*: there they went out of their way, and left their guide; for that place which should have been most holy, was now most vicious; the Church of God turned the Synagogue of Sathan; *Herod* himself their head, a Persecutor, where they thought to enquire; there they lost the sight of the starre (so he see more in *Fox.*) The false Church will never guide thee (by the bare notion) to the true Christ.

His inference comes to this, at last, (saith he) they found the Star, when they left *Jerusalem*, and left the false Church, and left the false Priests, and Scribes; and they no sooner turned their backs of *Jerusalem*, but immediately the Star appears to them again. All in a comfortable Letter to Mrs. Anne *Warcup*; If thou wouldest be guided to the true Christ, the true Jesus, he is not found among the rampant Clergy, or *Herodians*, but among his poor despised flock, the painful Shepherds that feed nigh the house of Bread (*i*) *Bethlehem*.

(*i*) 2 lost sight may again be recover'd, and the Star seen once again. But

But I only mention it for their sakes (poor Souls) that have lost the sight of their Jesus; Don't you often do so? Lord, (say some) I come to an Ordinance, and I have lost sight; and I come to the Table, or to Prayer, and I have lost sight; what shall I do? there's no outward Star, Ministry or Church can be a sufficient conduct; It is Jesus that must discover Jesus. Why then, you poor sinners, your way to attain true comfort, will be to attain a sight of Christ, by minding and following his own light, by which he leads and conducts; which is his Word, and his Spirit. Now there are two things more particularly, from whence consolation may be ministred.

First, Supposing that by these signatures God is about to produce some dreadful Judgment or other into the World, or into the Land? It was never known, (that I have yet read, in my small observation,) that such appearances or signs had not something signified by them, and sometimes, dreadful too. There is only one exception hinted before; the exception is that in 1186, there was a great conjunction of all the Planets in the Heavens, * in *September* 3*d*. and nothing followed it. There-

---

* *So S. Calvisus (said.)*

fore there is not dreadful things alwayes following such appearances, no more then Conjunctions: Dr. *Peter Serarius,* in a Book on Conjunctions, *pag.* 21, 22. writes the answer, consisting of four heads; one of which he notes at large: There were effects, (he denies the inference;) there were certainly various omens following that congress, tho' not in the same sign: in that year, (saith he) 1: A dreadful fiery beam was seen in the Heavens. 2. In *Italy* hail as big as Goose Eggs, 3. The *Cicilian* Sea went back, drown'd 5 millions of men. 4. *Carina* buried by an Earthquake. And 5. *Saladin* took *Jerusalem* from Christians. (He names four or five of them) very dreadful, (besides sickness, and the death of Princes, as before.) Then (saith he,) nothing at all is pleaded to have attended; but what Scripture (back't with good experience) allows of. Then certainly it concerns us to look about us: The sign, and the thing signified concur; admit the one, the other follows. Hence it concerns us, I say, to consider what we shall have to support us, if such Judgments come (as now are signified.) (*v*) but more likely to follow

---

(*v*) *And Gods wrath for them, if no signs at all appear'd.*

our

our sins, that procure them, so that the first branch of my use of consolation doeth respect evil to come, of which our sin is the cause, we neither believe God, nor his signs.

(Sæpe domi culpa est, nescimus credere cælo.)

And here *I* will (by Induction) say, if God should make fiery dreadful conflagrations to succeed this, which was the signature of some former Comets; the Issue of succeeding councels, present designs, and future changes in the world; will soon show: you know what terrible conflagrations we have had in this City; what abroad; what hath been *France*, *Holland*, *Flanders*, and *Germany*, tell; In one History I read; that there was a City * burnt, and there were certain Spirits seen strangely to move and run about in the Flames in the midst of the City. I do but alude to't and say whatsoever conflagrations were, — or are boding, look about you, there are certain Devilish Spirits going about in the world, that are designing to set the World, the Church on a flame, Heaven and Earth together. How shall

---

* P. Sera, *sayes* Constantinople *as I take it*.

we endeavour to comfort our selves in such fire? Why then I'le tell you, Do as *David* did: *Ziklag* was burnt, his Wives took Captive, and his Sons and Daughters; his Armies were discouraged, fired out of their quarters; and this, by the *Amalekites* too, the stock of *Edom*. (For, who are they, think you, but the *Romish* Edomites, that are for Fire-works?) Mark ye, what shall *David* do in this case? But *David* encouraged himself in the Lord his God. When all was burnt, he had a God that lived above, and governed the flames. 1 *Sam.* 30. 6. There's encouragement in God, (and cooling) for a drooping Spirit in the greatest burning flames in the World. Yea, when the greatest of all Fires, (that Spirituous Fire, that of the last day, the conflagration of Heaven and Earth shall be;) O how happy are they that have an interest in Christ, that can encourage themselves in the Lord, their God! That's one thing.

2. Is it Famine that God will plague our ryot, and excess by? * Then I'le say, in Famine he'l deliver thee from Death, *Job*. 5. 20. in War, from the Power of the

---

* *Many signs and Comets have often preceded it in all ages.*

Sword

Sword. And another promise saith, in the dayes of Famine, thou shalt be satisfied, *Psal.* 37. 19. and 111. 5. with Covenant Bread, *Isa.* 33. 16. Look how God fed the Widow, fed his poor Prophets, fed his poor destitute Saints; so now, look how God fed that famous Chaplain of the Admiral of *France*, (in the *Parisian* Massacre) Mr. *Merlin* by name, that made his escape upon a Hay-mow, a fortnight long: and how was he fed? A Hen came every day, and laid him an Egg; and this was the preservation of that good Chaplain: So in extraordinary cases, preternatural food comes as Mannah.

Sirs, if there be no ordinary, God will provide some extraordinary Pastures, that the very Ravens, (which are voracious) shall serve you, and feed you: Prodigious examples may testifie to Gods fidelity, and seal to our experience. Is it the Sword? What shall I mention? Is it the the Sword of a Forreigner? Is it the Sword of an intestine? Is it the Sword of persecution? Let whatsoever Sword will; be drawn; for Wars have frequently followed such dreadful signs in Heaven. There is comfort in this, that the God of peace is on your side; and if you perish in War outwardly, yet you may die in peace, (as *Josiah* did inwardly.) These

These are but three, of several instances, that *I* could easily have enlarged were it now needful. And if there be such matter of comfort, from the supposition of evils to come, what comfort may be expected, out of the good that comes after, that survivers may enjoy; in the conclusion light will follow; in the evening *Zach.* 14. 7. After which, more hopeful things may be expected to follow.

2d. *Branch,*
And what are those good issues that will end the Scene? I have observed in my little reading, there are nine stars recorded, (called Comets,) in the History of past times, and there have been wonderful glorious Issues, (or events of good) have followed them.

I'll begin with my text, (i'll but instance two or three, and reserve the rest for another place,) Christ Jesus now was an infant, (*) saith my Text, but he was born a King, I'll destroy him thinks *Herod*, Heark, but his languague was, I'll worship him. Well, the mother and babe, at the Purification escape that in *Jerusalem*: God contrives so, that *Joseph* (warn'd of God) carries the young child and his mother into *Egypt*: and so he escapes for some time

---

* 1. *Escapes may be obtained.*   there

there too: and shortly after, returns upon the message from God: *They are dead that sought the young childs life*; it seems then there were more then *Herod* that sought the destruction of Christ, (2 more of that name) and one may judge the *Herodian* (†) party very strong by this, there were a great many Executioners of those poor babes, that should have died with him, (rather than miss) but the plot would not take. Besides its thought he pleaded that old Prophesie, *Gen.* 49. 10. that he was that *Shilo*, or *Messias* that must come, the Scepter being gone from *Juda*. Why then, here's a good issue: it was a comfortable star yet it was dreadful to *Herod* and *Jerusalem*; a comfort to the babe, and wise men, and his (supposed) father *Joseph* and *Mary*; for they escaped, till *Herod* the Tyrant, (soon † after) was dead v. 19. And he dyed, saith *Josephus*, in the most horrible condition of body, as I have already touched.

There are some men, who seek to do all the mischief in the world they can, afore they dye, they dye under all the marks of God's vengeance upon them. So, that here's one effort of the star, though it appeared very low, yet it had high effects.

---

* *Godw.l.*1.13.*ch.* p.67 *Hebr.Antiquis.* † *Some say* 2 *years after.* 2. *Cap-*

2. *Captives*   A second is in my Text; *will return*   Captives may return home, for you see, though they were banished their own Countrey, as they in a sort were, yet they must return again, you may see it there, *v.* 29—23. So Mr. *Fox* at *Frankf.* said in a Sermon to the Exil'd ones you shall return now. She being dead that persecuted them, † Q. *Mary.*

3. *The Gospel will shine out.*   3*ly*. The glorious Sunlight of the Gospel will shine through all its clouds and dark parts; Christ and truth bear no long Eclipse.

The shining of the Sun (it is said in nature makes the rayes and beams of Comets (following it) so long and so large. Whatever it be in nature, this is certain, that the Sun shall run its course, and Christs train be very extensive. † When God is about to bring forth some great thing in the World, together with the evil preceeding, there shall good follow. A Glorious Sun of Righteousness shall arise at last, and *Sions* dark night shall end. There's comfort, as *Isai.* 60. 2. *ult.* Prodigious Comets are mostly night-sights, O when day-spring

---

† *Nec maris ac cœli spatium, nec terminus ævi finiet imperium.* Buchanon *in Psal.* 45.

visits us, *Zions* terror's over.

Fourthly, Reformation begun, will go on. I mean this, Reformation in the Worlds Laws, Renovation in the Church, *Acts* 3. 19. 21: God, (after such appearances) hath formerly in other Ages, used to raise up Instruments of Reformation, and to renew the Face of the World, and the Church; (all so wofully degenerated, and defac't I say) wofully. And mind it, stars are previous to all these; in experience. After one Star, (v) *Luther* appeared; after another (before that) (w) *John Wickliff* apeared; a Reformer; after other Stars other eminent instruments, (x) of glorious good in the world; *Zisca* happily fights the Emperour *Sigismund*; and the *Hussits* three times prevail. And so it was like a Resurrection of the Testimony of the Gospel, to the *Hussites* and *Bohemians*, after so great darkness of Popery and Tyranny. Why then, say I, by these small instances, (and, three or four more particulars noted in the end) you may conclude, that though things may look sad at first; Yet there are better things hoped for. Nay, the God of Heaven

---

(v) *Anno* 1516. (w) *Anno* 1363. (x) *Anno* 1400, 1401, 1402, 1403, *in all Comets do shine*

will

will set up a Kingdom, which shall not be shaken, nor delivered to other People. And these are the efforts and Issues of such glorious appearances. The King of the *Jews*, though he entred in the way of his cross, and is now gone to Heaven; when he returns again; he'l be exalted far above all Principalities and Powers.

And so the Doctrine of those false Astrologers came to nought. We find by one Author, that *Albumasar*, a great Astrologer and Magician did assert, that the Kingdom of Christ should come to nought about 900 years ago. It is now fifteen, sixteen hundred, and rising more and more, You see what a false Prophet he was. But the Gospel, and Doctrine, and Publishers of Gods holy will, shall rise and prosper, and so shall all they that love *Sion*.

Now for an Epilogue 3 or 4 hopeful things lighten the eyes of Protestants.

1. *Babylon* shall fall.
2. Great Oppressors must fall.
3. Glorious victories to the Saints.
4. The Kingdoms of this world shall fall to him, that was decreed and born to it.

1. *Babilon* must come down from her Luciferean pride, what that is in the letter,
Isa.

Isa. 13. and 14. chap. tell, (†) that *Roman* falſe, bewitching & poyſonful abyſſe as expounded by *John, Apoc.* 13. and to *John* cap. 17. that that whoriſh, (now withered) ſtrumpet of *Rome,* the ten horn'd beaſt that ſhe yet rides upon, and the unclean ſpirits, Prelates, Prieſts, Jeſuits, ſo abuſing the Kings of the earth *(*as the froggs*)* with their croaking; to trapan them into the battel of *Armageddon (*as once *Ahab* and *Joſias)* to their ruine, perſwading them to father, abet, or fauſter all her malice, Murthers and Maſſacres. This *Babilon* ſhall fall, not only here at home but at *Rome* alſo, *& mundi deſinet eſſe caput*; and look with what terror that *Roman* head looks on that late Comet (ſo Letters ſay) as boding that Hyerachical ſtate no good; ſo let them look the Lord God of recompences will in that Iſland, and of thoſe ten kingdomes, whom ſhe once uſurped and a late plotted to ruine, raiſe Inſtruments of her own to lay her naked, eat and burn her up.

Dr. *Tho Taylors* (*) Prophetie is then to take; Themſelves ſhall drink the blood intended againſt the woman, and root them

---

† *Of it a Sybil ſaid,* Roma ſhall be e'uen that is *a poor* Cottage, *then all her vile Maſſacres and Sorceries and burnings ſhall be laid open; to make the Nations abhor her.* *-*On* Apo. 12. *pag.* 816.

out

out, to make way for the Gospel in those desolate Popish Countreys; the time and their pride hastens it. So Mr. *Bur.* (*o*) to Dr. *Fearn* said, God will leave them to such Plots, that the Spirits of inferior Rulers shall execute due vengeance on them: then the multitude of her offences consumes the magnitude of her Forces: and it shall be easier for her to weigh the Mountains, measure the Fire, gather the Winds, or revive the verdour of wither'd grass, then to escape the judgment determined in its time. So *T. L.* said to *Q. E.* pag. 65.

2. Oppressors shall fall, they that did fell the Trees of the Forrest, spoyl'd the shade of the poor that shelter'd in distress under them, suffer'd no councels of Justice, peace, and relief to stand unfell'd by them, shall be themselves Subjects to the blow of Death, who equals Prince and Subjects. Now Mounsiers comes the diminution of your Glory.

Two things set Princes at odds below others, (to be admired) they might please to help it. (*) 1. Not stating the rights of Succession. And next, 2. (The reason of

---
(*o*) *Pag. the last, see also* Jo. Squire. *pag.* 626. *and also* F. L. *to* Q. Eliz. (p. 65. *on* Ap. 13.)
* *The Infirmity of* Q. *Elizabeth.*

the

the former) not admitting one Thought or Umbrage of Death to eclipse their myrth, (†)and so it comes surreptitiously on them of all men. Now their falls included in that of *Isai.* 13. 10, 11. and *v.* 19. 22. and for the lofty see *ch.* 14. 4, 5, so to 9. and 11, 12.— 19 — what that is to us? see *v.* 26. and it was in a year of Prodigies too, when *Ahaz* dyed, *v.* 28. the reason is, *v.* 32. for God has founded *Zion.* Read that of *Ezek.* (*) what cause of sighs, not mirth? (and especially to *Zedekiah's*,) now in him and his Brothers, the line was extinct: for treachery and oppressions, also that star in 1572 at first was fatal to the Protestants in *France, Quo plus sanguinis quàm vini fusum erat.* But *Ch.* the 9*th.* ended that bloody Scene in his own blood at last ; (†) For he dyed bleeding at all the Avenues of his body. So tragically did *Herod* in Diseases, end his rage *:* for the bloud of Infants, his sin and woe such (one seems, *Tragædia potius quam hystoria texi.*) *Lento igne corpus, urebatur,* &c. His Body as by gentle burning wasted his inwards, and so rabid, or voracious, no satisfying him

---

(†) *King* James. (*) Ezek. 21. 6, 10, 12, 15.
(†) Du' Serres. Enteb. p. 15. Joseph. Li. 17.
Antiqu.

with

with meats Inteſtines ulcerated: a lurid, and moiſt humor in his feet (*) ſwel'd all up from the lower parts: worms iſſued from his ſecrets, Spirits inflam'd; difficulty in breathing; worn with Tortures in all parts; all ſaid of him it was no other then *divinæ ultionis ſupplicium*: Gods heavy revenge, yet ſtill (in hope to live,) ſought Medicines, drunk waters, uſed ſuppleing oyls, and in that caſe his eyes being loſt, he wofully dyed. In *Math.* 2. 20. 'Tis ſaid they are dead, (not he only) it notes that the exit of cruel Tyrants, is often quick, ſeldom alone; they carry the Miniſters of their cruelty off with them and ſo are *tam pæna, quam culpæ participes*. This enſued on that Star the like has often ſince.

3. Glorious victories, (one eſpecially) on the ſide of the Lamb, and his followers, will end all, and ſucceed the Stars (and more brisk Comets perhaps, (s) come) as they preceed the Wars: We have had *bellum Ethnicum*, an Heathen-War in the Emperours, and papal in the Popes: alſo (here in *Brit.*) *Bellum Epiſcopale*, in late times; *& Presbyteriale*, &c. and all had

---

(*) *Humor luridus.* (†) *Has pænas divinitus ob geſta ejus impie depoſui.* (s) *Til that laſt Star of Jacob the ſign and thing ſignify'd come.*

their

their fucceffive victories. One war I look for yet in the valley of *Jehofophat*, (as Sir H. V. faid,) that brings the deciding judgment of God; (as *Joel* 3 13.) and that ends *Zion* controverfie fully, till that *Bellum Gogo-Mogogicum* comes *Apoc.* 20. Now this is at the Refurrection of the witneffes, and fix Vial; that *Bellum agninum*, *Apoc.* 17. 14. reported, Chap. 19. 11. And to this belongs one more, *victoria Haleluiiatica* * (for us *Brittains*) then all weapons are to ceafe, and turn tools for culture, as *Ifa.* 2. 4. *Mic* 4. 3. *Ezek.* 39. 9, 12. or at laft be burnt : (that will be a work of fome time, feven years, but the burials are over in feven moneths, ver. 12.) let the Saints hold what battel they will, Conquerers they fhall be, nay more then Conquerors they be, nay more then fo, *Rom* 8. 37. in their Captain, and fome way in themfelves, they're victors, *Col.* 2. 15. (at laft as Chrift was) by, and in their deathes; Nay in all external conflicts too, at long run, (as of *Gad*, *Gen* 49. 19.) a Troop may overcome, yet he overcame at laft. Except that onely of the witneffes, *Rev.* 11. 7. and that onely for three years and an half; and yet the Refurrection gives it them after.

If seditions, murders, and assassinations (more private) or Tumults, Massacres, Invasions and Insurrections do befall *Brittan* or *Ireland*; now again by that rampant (I mean) *French* Tyrant (our *Assyrian*,) as once *Turks* in *Hungary* after a Comet, and we in *England*, (after another) *Faliciter pugnatum erit* (as one said) the victory will be ours: tho' I deny not but God may plague us with *French* and Papal Factions, for our *Fr.* and Antiparliamentary fashions; if any wish it *al-a-mode*, they may in *Jam.* the 2*d.* have their wish: and yet a party is extant, that may try the truth, and plead the justice of our Cause, Religion and Laws as warmly (and to the same purpose) as in *Smithfield* by a Fagot. (*o*) Time was, the *French* Mounsier was often fairly beat by the *English* on his own Ground. If now in defence of a Papal head, (forrein or domestick,) he shall put Protestants in our own land, to a just self-defence, tho' he may fish a while in our puddl'd waters, and take advantage of our divisions to divide the spoyl of the first Battel; yet let him look for a fresh rancounter by a (*)

(*o*) 1 Speed *Chron. in H.* 5. *p.* 781. * Speed *Anno* 1348 *Edw.* 3 *p.* 654.

reserved

reserved and resolv'd Party, that will bark at an Alien, (and bite too) as hard as any of old *Nols* Curs ever did; that had both him, and his Councels once in awe.

4ly, The Kingdoms of this world fall to Chrisfs possession: (right he had long since;) *Psal.*2. 9, 10. not only of that ultimate glory in heaven, but to raign on the earth. *Apoc.* 5. 10. this *Virgil* calls *Saturnium regnum*: (*) and so do the *Sybils*: (*i.e.*) the golden age, when wisdom and knowledge will be the stability of our times, and strength of Salvation, *Isa.* 33.6. I grant, 't has had its eruptions in all ages by past, even when *Amaleck* laid hands on the throne, *Exod.* 17. 16., yea under the Cross, so that they had almost forc't the crown on him by surprize (ere he suffer'd,) *Joh.* 6. 15. and Christ owns the Kingdom point, to be a truth, Chap. 18. 37. tho (then) not of this world, yet to be (now) in it. Nor were the *Magi* gull'd by this star: If born a King, sure Christ has a real Kingdom, not barely titular: for Comets speak of no shams. By't I mean three things.

1. That Christ *de jure*, is the King of Na-

---

* *On this golden age that shall revolve in the last of the last times.*

tions, as well as Saints, *Jer.* 10. 7. 10. and ought *de facto* so to be proclaimed over the world, (as well as in the Church) that in all he may have preheminence, *Col.* 1. 18.

2. That his Laws declar'd in the word, (and not repeal'd) ought to be the municipal Laws to the world, (as to the Church) and all contrary to plain *Scripture* ought to be rescinded, and vacate, in all our Courts.

3. That his people (*i.e.*) (that are able, fear God, hate covetousness;) ought to Minister those Laws, and for him, execute justice to all oppress't, and on oppressors, for this medicine Nations are sick, and must never beheal'd without it: on such substrata's ought our Constitutions to build, that would not incurr the weight of Chrifts Iron rod, so would that Prophesie obtain in all lands; the Kingdoms of this world be the Lords: that *T. L.* (*o*) sayes were so long usurped by Monarchs and Antichrist, that of right by Lordship and Inheritance, did ever belong to God, and the Prince of the Covenant, shall be restored to their right owner: Of which Kingdom shall be n finis.

(*o*) *Rev.* 11. 15. *See* T. L. p. 15 *on that Prophesie.*

When

When

Righteousness ascends the highest Throne
And faith with Reason, shall agree in one,
And all the virtues to their Councel call,
Cabals and vicious Councellors shall fall.

Exque polo veniet rex, tempus in omne futurum, &c. * In all, the scope is, to show the tremendous signs that precede the second coming of Christ. One *Scheltcon* of *Embden* writ on that subject in 1577, two year after that new star (in *Cassiopea*) as the Messenger or warner of Christs judgment. † *Serarius* a late, and before *Cyprian Leovit.* 1583, wrote of a famous Conjunction of the superior Planets, in the end of *Piscis*, as (says he) six years before the first coming of Christ, a star, and that same Conjunction appear'd; so at's second, &c. then Cites the verses of *Jo. Stoffler* in *Melancthon*. Of that Star in *Cassiopea*'s Chair, writ *Tycho Brahe*.

One *John Bainbrigg* (in K. *James*'s time) writ Learnedly of that star in 1618. he (pag. 31.) calls it an heavenly harbinger that did presignifie the glorious light of the

---

* S*y*bil Erithr. accrosticks.   † Pag. 11, 12, &c.
So also did Theod. Beza in's verses.

Gospel to shine to the whole world, and that in 1558 was a sign of good to poor Protestants in *Brittany*, *Germany*, and that *France*, &c. should yet again flourish.

Then peace and knowledge of the truth, shall flourish,
The earth her plentious fruits shall also cherish;
It shall not be divided as before,
Nor to the plow be subject any more.

To conclude if such judgments may be attended with mercies, such signs of usual evil, may precede, (presignifie) much good, If bad signs at present, may be glad significations, for the future: In a word, if the first *Epiphany* of Christ to the Sages, (and under the Cross) did by a star so irradiate the very East, as to call them out so far to visit his manger, and stable: Oh with what dazling Luster will his second part of the Kingdoms Epiphany be attended? to the joy of the upright, the terrour of all cruel *Herodians*, shame of Apostate Jews, and (finally) to the gathering of all to behold his rising Sun-light. Amen, Lord come quickly.

† *See more in* pag. 32. &c. *of Bainbr.*

To put my self and the reader in tune again, if weary with reading (as I am in writing) let him warble over the two or three Hymnes for a conclusion of this starry Treatise.

Our Lord after the cup sung one; what a one, 'tis not said. The late sweet usage of Hymnes (as was among the old Church) observ'd in *Eusebius*; now seems to revive in our Assemblies (and to be wisht in our Famelies too) Mr. *Hen. Jessy* left a sweet one in print yet not forgot. It begun thus,

Lord hast to bring Mount Zions King,
Unto his promis't Throne.
By Royal right, birth, purchase, fight,
All Kingdoms are his own, &c.

One Col. *Jo. Fenwick* in his *Zions* joy in her King, pag. 92, 93, &c. on *Psal.* 102. has another too, that may be seen at large in that book, *An.* 1643. May I then propose (not Impose) my Hymnes (two or three of them, for a tast) first to the reading then to serve the Religious joy of any, that desire to obey them Scriptures in *Eph.* and *Colos.* and I may (if these be accepted well) give the reader a larger Volume in time.

When

1. When God shall Christ his Son anoint,
    On Zions holy hill;
Salvation thence he will appoint,
    For walls and Bulwarks still.
The great shall then no terrour be,
    The good to over-awe;
And force them into corners flee,
    For keeping of Gods Law.

The vile no more account shall bear,
    Tyrants no more oppress;
No piercing bramble, just ones tear;
    None, rise by wickedness.
But right, and truth ascends the Throne;
    To 'ffront Iniquity;
And reason, justice, faith, in one
    United; shall agree.

Then worship pure, shall not endure,
    Foggs Superstitious;
Nor Scarlet whore, shall more allure
    To Babel, for Gods house.
Scripture our Royal guide, and Law
    The word, the sword shall blunt.
Vengeance shall Hornes and Myters saw.
    The Nimrods, cease to hunt.

Thus Heav'n, and Earth, to joy shall break,
    (A joy that ends distress,)
He for the meek, will judgment seek,
    And hasten righteousness.
                    Amen.

2. *To God let's all sing praise*
That by his word all made,
Thus Heav'n above; and all that move
On Earth, their being had.
For Sun that lights the day,
For Moon and glittering stars,
That in the night foreshew us light,
(As signs) of peace or wars.

For th' earth and all its hosts,
The sea and what's therein,
All subject stand, by Gods command
To man: thats fallen by sin.
For hail, and rain, and dew,
For stormy winds also;
For these fulfil Gods righteous will,
When men against it, go.

For day, and also night,
Summer, and winter's frost:
(Contraries do, Gods wisdom show,
And oft profit us most.)
But Lord whats fall'n man?
Dominion such to have,
Or'e all things here; and tryumph there
With Christ, ore death and grave.

Consume Lord from thy earth
Destructive wicked men;
Oh come again, resume thy raign;
Come quickly! Lord Amen.
                              · *Halelujah.*

3. *Thy glory Lord the Heavens on high*
    And Firmament declares.
Yea all their hoasts thee magnifie,
    Consorting with the stars.
The brightness, number, Influence,
    Of starry skyes proclaim,
Their makers skill and excellence,
    That gives them all their name.

Sometimes (for God) they battles fight,
    And (in their course) declare,
The deaths, and woes, of men of might
    That great oppressors are.
At first, creation, then behold!
    These sons of God all sing,
A new star Christ, to th' wise men told
    Born to the Jews, a King.

Such new and dreadful sights portend,
    What shall this world affright:
When Jesus shall again descend
    To judge and save the upright.
Thou Star of Jacob; rise, appear,
    Come bright and morning Star;
Irradiate, our dark hemisphere,
    O bee'nt so long, so far.

Thy rising brings Brittans *day-spring,*
    And fright Herodians *proud;*
Then Sons of God again shall sing,
    Lord hast, shine through the cloud.

FINIS.   Amen.

www.ingramcontent.com/pod-product-compliance
Lightning Source LLC
Chambersburg PA
CBHW020310170426
43202CB00008B/562